The Boo

B.S.A.
(GROUPS B. AND M.)

A PRACTICAL GUIDE ON THE HANDLING AND
MAINTENANCE OF ALL 1955 TO 1967 FOUR-
STROKE O.H.V. SINGLES, EXCEPT ALL 250 c.c.,
"GOLD STAR" AND B44 "VICTOR" MODELS

BY

W. C. HAYCRAFT
F.R.S.A.

ANNOUNCEMENT

By special arrangement with the original publishers of this book, Sir
Isaac Pitman & Son, Ltd., of London, England, we have secured the exclusive
publishing rights for this book, as well as all others in THE MOTORCYCLIST'S
LIBRARY.

Included in THE MOTORCYCLIST'S LIBRARY are complete instruction manuals covering the care and operation of respective motorcycles and engines;
valuable data on speed tuning, and thrilling accounts of motorcycle race
events. See listing of available titles elsewhere in this edition.

We consider it a privilege to be able to offer so many fine titles to our
customers.

FLOYD CLYMER
Publisher of Books Pertaining to Automobiles and Motorcycles

2125 W. PICO ST.   LOS ANGELES 6, CALIF.

INTRODUCTION

Welcome to the world of digital publishing ~ the book you now hold in your hand, while unchanged from the original edition, was printed using the latest state of the art digital technology. The advent of print-on-demand has forever changed the publishing process, never has information been so accessible and it is our hope that this book serves your informational needs for years to come. If this is your first exposure to digital publishing, we hope that you are pleased with the results. Many more titles of interest to the classic automobile and motorcycle enthusiast, collector and restorer are available via our website at **www.VelocePress.com.** We hope that you find this title as interesting as we do.

NOTE FROM THE PUBLISHER

The information presented is true and complete to the best of our knowledge. All recommendations are made without any guarantees on the part of the author or the publisher, who also disclaim all liability incurred with the use of this information.

TRADEMARKS

We recognize that some words, model names and designations, for example, mentioned herein are the property of the trademark holder. We use them for identification purposes only. This is not an official publication.

INFORMATION ON THE USE OF THIS PUBLICATION

This manual is an invaluable resource for the classic **BSA** enthusiast and a "must have" for owners interested in performing their own maintenance. However, in today's information age we are constantly subject to changes in common practice, new technology, availability of improved materials and increased awareness of chemical toxicity. As such, it is advised that the user consult with an experienced professional prior to undertaking any procedure described herein. While every care has been taken to ensure correctness of information, it is obviously not possible to guarantee complete freedom from errors or omissions or to accept liability arising from such errors or omissions. Therefore, any individual that uses the information contained within, or elects to perform or participate in do-it-yourself repairs or modifications acknowledges that there is a risk factor involved and that the publisher or its associates cannot be held responsible for personal injury or property damage resulting from the use of the information or the outcome of such procedures.

One final word of advice, this publication is intended to be used as a reference guide, and when in doubt the reader should consult with a qualified technician.

PREFACE

THE author's aim in compiling this maintenance handbook is to provide *all* essential data and instructions necessary for owners of popular "B" and "M" group B.S.A. O.H.V. singles to obtain and sustain maximum m.p.g., m.p.h., r.p.m., b.h.p. and pleasure from their attractive and reliable mounts.

This final edition supersedes and is more comprehensive throughout than the preceding 16th edition. It deals with the efficient *handling and maintenance*, but *not* major overhaul of the following 1955-67 four-stroke singles—

1. The 1955-9 348 c.c. O.H.V. Models B31, and B32.
2. The 1955-60 499 c.c. O.H.V. Models B33, and B34.
3. The 1955-8 499 c.c. O.H.V. Model M33.
4. The 1955-8 499 c.c. O.H.V. Model M33.
5. The 1961-7 343 c.c. O.H.V. "Star" Models B40, and B40 SS90.

The B31-B34 engine range is of identical design to the M33 engine, but entirely different from the B40 range. Models B40 and B40 SS90 were both produced throughout 1965, but Model B40 SS90 was discontinued for 1966 and Model B40 continued for export only during 1966-7.

B.S.A. models *not* dealt with in this handbook are: the "Gold Star" O.H.V. singles; the "Bantam" two-stroke singles; the four-stroke 250 c.c. O.H.V. singles; the A7 and A10 type O.H.V. vertical twins; the A50 and A65 type O.H.V. vertical twins; and the B44 "Victor" O.H.V. singles. All except the first and last mentioned are dealt with in separate Pitman handbooks.

In conclusion, the author would make clear that *all* maintenance instructions in this handbook where *not* specifically dated apply to 1955 onwards and to all machines except B.S.A. models to which specific reference *is* made. He also sincerely thanks B.S.A. Motor Cycles Ltd. of Armoury Road, Birmingham, 11 (Phone: *VIC 2381*), Joseph Lucas Ltd., and Amal Ltd., both also of Birmingham, for kindly supplying miscellaneous technical data and for permitting him to reproduce various copyright illustrations.

Bedford Row,   W. C. Haycraft
Worthing, Sussex.

CONTENTS

CHAPTER 1

HANDLING A B.S.A.

IT is not possible in this maintenance handbook to deal with actual riding except in the briefest outline and considerations of space at the author's disposal make it necessary for him to concentrate on the layout and handling of B.S.A. controls and to omit dealing with the technique of riding, legal matters, etc. Do not fail to read copies of the 6d. official booklets, *The Highway Code* and *The New Traffic Signs*. Also always wear a crash helmet while riding.

The Riding Position. The standard riding position on a new B.S.A. is generally found to be satisfactory for a man of average build, but to suit those not of average physique, a combined adjustment of the handlebars, footrests, and some of the handlebar controls, can be made. See that the riding position is really comfortable. The footrest hanger bosses are serrated internally and the hangers can be moved to alternative positions. The handlebars are readily adjustable (four bolts). A shaped foam-rubber pad beneath a saddle top improves comfort.

LAYOUT AND USE OF CONTROLS

The controls (mostly on the handlebars) may conveniently be divided into three groups: (1) engine controls, (2) motor-cycle controls, and (3) electrical controls. Before attempting to start up, you should, if you have never previously handled a B.S.A., get quite familiar with the controls.

It is assumed that you are familiar with general principles and understand the functions of the controls which are more or less the same on all motor-cycles. If you are a complete novice it is a good plan to sit on the saddle and "twiddle" the various levers while thinking about what would happen if the engine were running.

On "Magdyno" Models. The layout of the handlebar controls is clearly shown in Fig. 1. This layout applies to all 1955–7 "Magdyno" models; there is some variation in the positions of the speedometer, ammeter, and lighting switch.

Those handling a B.S.A. for the first time should note the following points—

1. All handlebar controls (excluding 1955–6 ignition levers) are operated by *inward* movement.

2. The throttle twist-grip (which controls engine speed) has a full movement of approximately *one-quarter* of a complete turn. With the throttle-stop correctly set to provide good tick-over, the throttle slide does not close completely. On most B.S.A. models it is essential to use a very small throttle opening (about one-sixteenth to one-eighth of the total twist-grip movement) for starting from cold; otherwise some difficulty may be experienced.

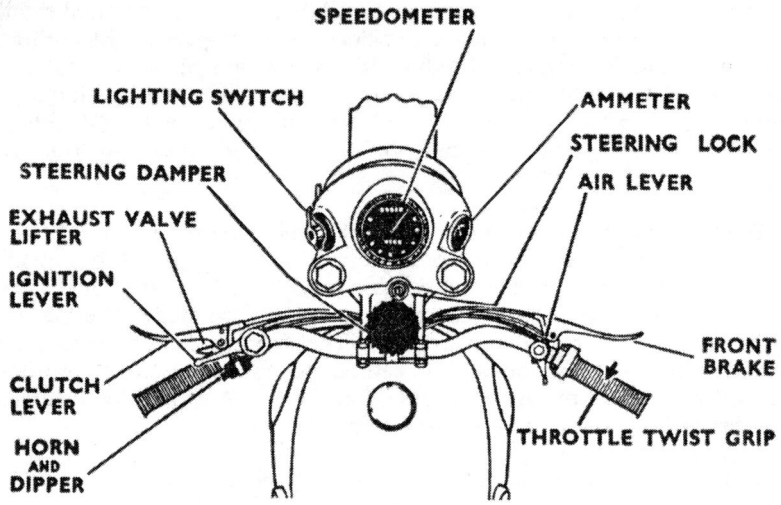

Fig. 1. Layout of Handlebar Controls, etc., on
1955–7 O.H.V. "Magydyno" Models

The steering lock (operated by a Yale key) was introduced in 1955. On 1955 models
the horn and dipper switches were separate.

3. The air lever (which enables the mixture of air and petrol to be varied) must be kept closed completely for starting from *cold* but at all other times it should normally be *wide open*. Slight closing when travelling slowly under load, to ward off a tendency for pinking, may sometimes be desirable, but it is generally best to use the ignition lever to forestall pinking.

4. The ignition lever (which moves the contact-breaker base on the magneto portion of the "Magdyno") should always be kept fully, or nearly fully, advanced while riding, except when pinking occurs. For pinking, less frequent now with branded fuels, the ignition should be temporarily retarded a shade, but note that this automatically reduces the power output. At the first opportunity after temporary retardation, the ignition lever should be *advanced as far as possible*. For starting

purposes, however, it is always advisable to retard the ignition lever slightly to prevent the risk of kick-back.

5. Never use the exhaust-valve lifter (which raises the exhaust-valve off its seat) for any purpose other than starting and stopping the engine. It is permissible, however, to use it occasionally when descending hills, provided that the throttle is shut right back and the air lever is kept wide open.

6. The clutch lever (which disconnects and re-connects the drive from the engine to the rear wheel) must always be used *fully* and *progressively*. Use it only when moving off and during each gear change. For comfort, slip some rubber tube on to the lever (also the front-brake lever).

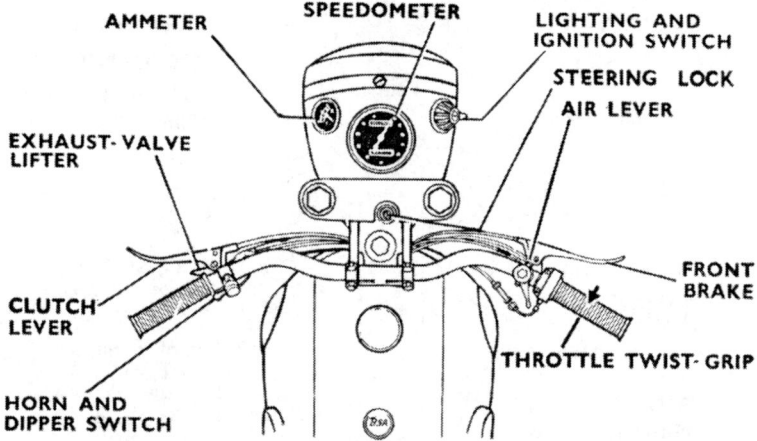

FIG. 2. LAYOUT OF HANDLEBAR CONTROLS, ETC., ON 1958–60 COIL IGNITION O.H.V. MODELS B31, B32, B33, B34

The 1958–60 350 c.c. and 500 c.c. O.H.V. models with Lucas alternator and rectifier (instead of a "Magdyno") have no ignition lever, but an ignition switch.

7. The foot gear-change pedal on the off-side of the gearbox provides four gear ratios and "neutral" which lies between first and second gears. Note that "neutral" can only be obtained *after* engaging first gear. All downward changes (*see* Fig. 4) are made by upward movement of the pedal with the toe, and all upward changes are made by downward movement of the toe. The gear-change pedal returns to the same (horizontal) position after each gear change is effected, ready for the next change to be made. During each gear change it is necessary to make a *full* movement of the gear-change pedal.

On Coil Ignition Models B31–B34. The control layout for Models B31–B34 is shown in Fig. 2. No ignition lever is provided, the advance and retard being automatically controlled. An ignition key is provided in the centre of the lighting switch mounted on the off-side of the headlamp cowl. It has three positions: EMG (emergency), OFF, and IGN (ignition on). The EMG and IGN positions are on the left- and right-hand sides respectively of the OFF position.

In the event of the battery being exhausted, the engine can be started after temporarily turning the ignition key to the EMG position. Starting

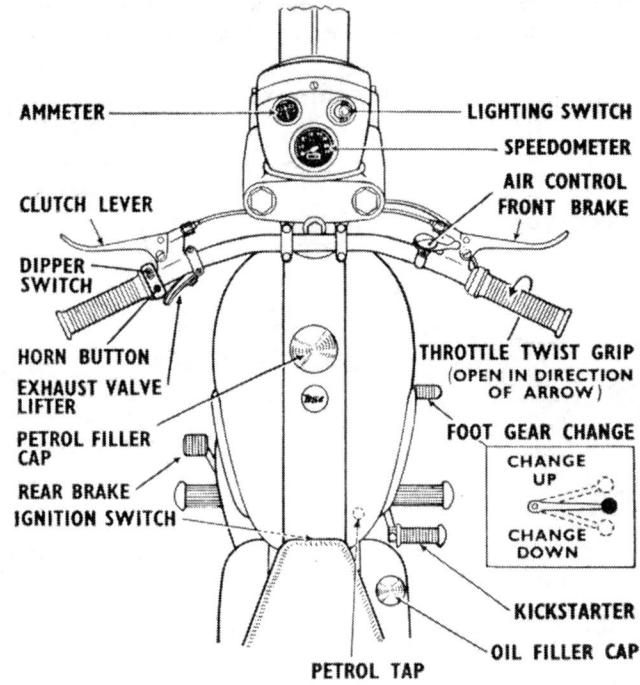

FIG. 3. LAYOUT OF HANDLEBAR CONTROLS, ETC., ON 1961–6
COIL IGNITION O.H.V. MODELS B40, B40 SS90

is normally effected with the ignition key turned to the IGN position. Whenever the engine is stopped, the key should be turned to the OFF position to prevent battery discharge.

On Coil Ignition Models B40, B40 SS90. The handlebar control layout for Model B40 is shown in Fig. 3. It is very similar to the B31 to B34 layout, but there is no ignition key provided in the centre of the lighting switch. The ignition switch is mounted on the fairing immediately behind the engine and has three positions: Ignition, Off, and Emergency. Before an attempt is made to start the engine the switch should be turned to the "IGN" position, but if for some reason the battery is exhausted the switch should be turned to the "EMG" position for starting. It should be rapidly turned to the central "IGN" position as soon as the engine runs at a moderate speed.

An alternative switch has a detachable key at its centre. When the key is in a horizontal position the ignition is switched off. To switch on the ignition, turn the key *clockwise*. The emergency starting position is obtained by depressing the key and turning *anti-clockwise* from the central position. The ignition must always be switched off when the motor-cycle is left with the engine stopped.

Modified Petrol Tap. On all 1955–7 "Magdyno" models and the 1958–60 Models B31–B34 to turn the push-and-pull type petrol tap on or off, pull the serrated button out or push it in respectively. To switch over to the reserve petrol supply from the main supply, turn the button *clockwise* and pull it out about ⅛ in. further to lock it (*see* page 9).

Starting Up. Before attempting to start up, make quite sure that there is sufficient engine oil of the correct type and grade in the oil tank, gearbox, and oil-bath chain case (*see* Chapter IV), and that the motor-cycle parts have been adequately lubricated, and the battery attended to.

The oil tank has a maximum capacity of 4 to 5½ pints (according to the machine). Also check that the tyre pressures (*see* page 107) are correct and that there is sufficient petrol in the tank, the capacity of which varies from 3 to 4 gal.

Push your B.S.A. forward off its rear or centre stand, or keep it jacked up. If the machine is moved off its stand it is advisable to stand astride the machine, as this helps to balance it. Turn on the petrol tap.

On a coil ignition model always verify that the ignition is switched on. On a "Magdyno" or coil model with a separate air lever, close this completely if starting from *cold*, and retard the ignition lever (where fitted) so that it is about half fully advanced.

Open the throttle very slightly (say, one-eighth) by *inward* movement of the throttle twist-grip. See that the foot gear-change mechanism is in "neutral," i.e. between first and second gears. It is advisable actually to verify that the operation of the kick-starter does not rotate the wheel. If the engine is quite cold, momentarily depress the tickler on the carburettor float-chamber, but do not flood the carburettor so that petrol begins to drip. If the engine is warm, do not flood the carburettor at all, and leave the air lever (where fitted) partly (say, one-third) open. *Now start up.*

Depress the kick-starter slowly until you feel the resistance of engine compression, raise the exhaust-valve lifter, and then give the kick-starter pedal a vigorous downward kick. At the same time release the exhaust-valve lifter. The engine should start up at the first or second attempt, but if it fails to do so, repeat the starting procedure. As soon as the engine of a "Magdyno" model fires, advance the ignition lever fully, or nearly fully. Now open the air lever slowly as far as possible until the engine runs evenly at a moderate speed.

Engaging First Gear. Disengage the clutch by squeezing the handlebar lever, and move the foot gear-change pedal *upwards* to its *full* extent (*downwards* on Models B40, B40 SS90). If you fail to engage first gear readily with the motor-cycle stationary, rock the machine gently to and fro while maintaining slight pressure on the foot gear-change pedal. Continue doing this until you *feel* that first gear is engaged.

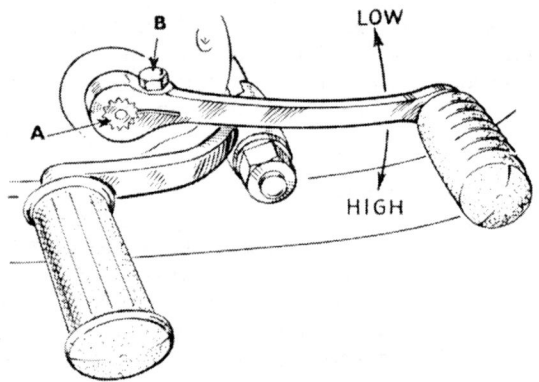

FIG. 4. THE B.S.A. POSITIVE-STOP FOOT GEAR-CHANGE

After making each gear change, the lever and pedal always return to the same position. The lever is adjustable on the splined shaft *A* after loosening the pinch-bolt *B*.

Moving Off. Open the throttle slightly by turning the throttle twist-grip *inwards*, and gently and progressively engage the clutch by releasing the handlebar lever. As the clutch engages and the motor-cycle gathers momentum, open the throttle a little more. Should any slight pinking occur, on a "Magdyno" model, immediately retard the ignition very slightly, or close the air lever a shade. For all normal running after the engine has warmed up it is important to keep the ignition lever fully advanced ("Magdyno" models) and the air lever wide open, so long as this does not entail any tendency for the engine to "knock."

Making Upward Gear Changes. Momentarily close the throttle, disengage the clutch, and *depress* (*raise* on Models B40, B40 SS90) the foot gear-change pedal to its *full* extent. As far as possible, combine these three actions in one *smooth* movement. Pause a second before disengaging the clutch. Quickly but progressively re-engage the clutch and simultaneously open the throttle again, immediately the desired gear change is effected. When changing up into second, third, or fourth gear, avoid imposing undue pressure on the foot gear-change pedal, because this can cause damage and is quite unnecessary, but maintain light pressure until the clutch is re-engaged.

Making Downward Gear Changes. Simultaneously open the throttle slightly, pause a second, disengage the clutch, and with toe pressure *raise:* (*depress* on Models B40, B40 SS90) the foot gear-change pedal to its full extent. Then quickly and progressively re-engage the clutch.

When making a gear change, hold the foot gear-change pedal in position with the toe until the gear is *felt* to engage and the clutch has been re-engaged. Make all gear changes quietly and smoothly. An accomplished motor-cyclist does not advertise to the whole street that he is making a gear change.

Note that when changing down quickly from fourth or third gear into first gear it is not essential to disengage the clutch, to throttle up the engine and to *re-engage the clutch* during each gear change. It is sufficient to slow down to a low speed, disengage the clutch, and make two or three full upward (downward on Models B40, B40 SS90) movements of the gear-change pedal in quick succession, according to whether third or fourth gear respectively was previously engaged. Each time you raise the gear-change pedal "blip" the engine, i.e. throttle up slightly.

To Obtain "Neutral." It is necessary to change down into first gear, stop,* and then with the clutch still disengaged, *slightly* and very gently *depress* (*raise* on Models B40, B40 SS90) the foot gear-change pedal with the toe. In this instance do not move the pedal to its full extent, otherwise you will miss "neutral" and engage second gear. A "light touch" is required, and you should be careful to re-engage the clutch gradually in case first gear should have been accidentally engaged.

To Stop the Machine. Close the throttle, apply both brakes simultaneously, and change down into neutral.

To Stop the Engine. With neutral engaged and the throttle shut right back (giving generally a slow tick-over), raise the exhaust-valve lifter, or (on coil-ignition models) switch off the ignition.

Run in Engine Carefully for 1,000–1,500 Miles. *The advice given here is the most important advice in the book.* Except with bench-tested "Gold

---

* A really accomplished rider can obtain "neutral" *before* coming to a complete standstill, but a novice is not advised to attempt to obtain "neutral" while the machine is moving.

Star" engines, all new or reconditioned power-units must be handled with great care for the first 1,000–1,500 miles. Attend to all routine maintenance operations with special care. After covering 250 miles drain and refill the oil tank with suitable oil and clean the filters (*see* pages 40, 41). Repeat this at 500 miles and thereafter every 2,000 miles. Change the gearbox oil after the first 500 miles and then every 5,000 miles (*see* page 44).

During the running-in period the throttle should not be opened wide; a new or reconditioned engine should be nursed very carefully, otherwise it may be permanently spoiled and never deliver its full power. When new, bearing surfaces appear dead smooth but actually they are covered with fine tool marks which are invisible to the naked eye. Until these disappear, and a mirror-like gloss and hardness spread all over, local friction is very apt to occur and the oil film may break down at one or more places, possibly causing a seizure. To speed on a new machine is a great temptation, but for some time, be content with *one-third* of full throttle and always avoid rapid acceleration.

Make a point of not using more than *half* throttle in any gear until running-in is nearly completed. Avoid rapid acceleration and by making full use of the gearbox, aim at making the engine run "light" as much as possible. As the running-in period nears completion, progressively increase the throttle openings, but do not run on full throttle until 1,500 miles have been covered.

During Running-in. Avoid rapid acceleration, particularly if the engine is not pulling under load, and above all never allow the engine to labour when hill climbing through not changing down to a lower gear in good time.

Check the various routine adjustments (*see* Chapter V) such as plug and contact-breaker gaps, tappet clearances, clutch adjustment, etc., somewhat more often than usual, and also check external nuts and bolts for tightness (*see* page 54). *Always keep the oil tank well topped-up* (*see* page 35), and change the engine oil, clean the tank filter and change the gearbox oil at the periods previously specified.

Use Upper-cylinder Lubricant during Running-in Period. B.S.A. Motor Cycles, Ltd., recommend the addition during running-in of some upper-cylinder lubricant to the *petrol* each time the tank is replenished. Where an upper-cylinder lubricant such as "Redex" is not available, it is wise to add about one egg-cupful of engine oil to every two gallons of petrol.

The Speedometer Trip. To turn the trip to zero, pull out the spring-loaded flexible control under the instrument and turn it *clockwise*. On releasing the control, it automatically disengages.

Steering Head Lock. All 1955 and later models have a thief-proof locking device built into the steering head. To lock the steering when parking the machine, insert the Yale key into the key-hole (*see* Fig. 1) and turn the key when the steering is moved over to the *left* to almost its full extent. Be very careful not to lose the key (always keep it on a chain ring), and note the important advice on page 47 regarding the application of oil.

Modified Petrol Tap. On the 1961–6 343 c.c. "Star" Models B40 and B40 SS90 the petrol tap is located as shown in Fig. 3. To turn on the petrol, pull out the serrated button fully and lock it in this position by turning the button *anti-clockwise*. To turn off the petrol, turn the button *clockwise* and push it right home. Somewhat different petrol taps are fitted to 1955–60 348 and 499 c.c. O.H.V. models and these are briefly referred to on page 5.

CHAPTER II

ALL ABOUT CARBURATION

ALL B.S.A. models are sent out from the works with the carburettors carefully tuned and with jet sizes, throttle valve, and needle position giving the best all-round performance. Normally it is not wise to alter the maker's setting. A slow-running adjustment is, however, sometimes required and after a considerable mileage it may be desirable to alter the jet needle position. About every six months the carburettor should be dismantled, thoroughly cleaned, and inspected.

This chapter deals with the "Monobloc" type Amal instrument. Some understanding of how the Amal carburettor functions is desirable.

"MONOBLOC" TYPE AMAL CARBURETTOR

Functioning of Instrument. The "Monobloc" type Amal carburettor differs from the standard type of instrument used on S.V. and O.H.V. singles prior to 1955 in several fairly important respects, but its general functioning is similar. The "Monobloc" design includes: a horizontal float chamber made integral with the carburettor body; a float needle of moulded nylon; a top petrol-feed; a needle jet with "bleed" holes giving two-way compensation; and a detachable pilot jet which can be easily cleaned.

Fig. 5 illustrates the essential parts of the instrument. The float chamber (13) and float needle (9) maintain a constant level of petrol in the needle-jet (14) and the pilot jet (17). The selection by the makers of the appropriate jet sizes and main-bore choke ensures a proper atomizing and proportioning of the petrol and air sucked into the engine.

KEY TO FIG. 5

1. Mixing-chamber cap	14. Needle-jet
2. Mixing-chamber cap ring	15. Main-jet holder
3. Air valve	16 Main jet
4. Jet-needle clip	17. Pilot jet
5. Jet block	18. Throttle-stop adjusting screw
6. Air passage to pilot jet	19. Jet block locating-screw
7. Tickler assembly	20. Pilot air-adjusting screw
8. Banjo securing-bolt	21. Mixing chamber
9. Float needle	22. Fibre seal
10. Float	23. Jet needle
11 Float-chamber cover screws	24. Throttle valve
12. Float-chamber cover	25. Throttle return-spring
13. Float chamber	

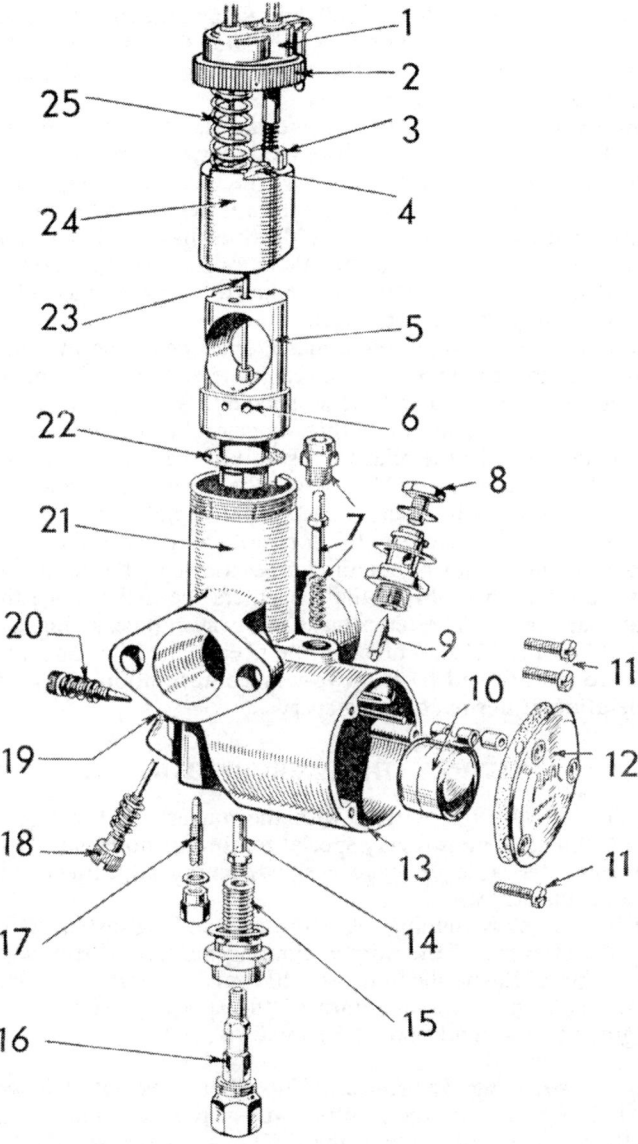

FIG. 5. EXPLODED VIEW OF 1955–66 AMAL "MONOBLOC" CARBURETTOR
Some later models have a rubber "O" ring on the carburettor flange.

The air valve (3) is normally kept fully raised, and the throttle valve (24), controlled by the handlebar twist-grip, regulates the volume of mixture, and therefore the power. At all throttle openings a correct mixture is automatically obtained.

The "Monobloc" type carburettor, like the standard type instrument, operates in four stages. When opening the throttle from the fully closed position to one-eighth open (for tick-over) the mixture is supplied by the pilot jet (17), and the strength of the mixture is determined by the setting of the knurled pilot air-adjusting screw (20) which has a coil locking-spring to facilitate adjustment. As the throttle is opened slightly farther, the main jet system comes into action, the mixture being augmented by the main jet (16) through the pilot by-pass.

The amount of cut-away on the atmospheric side of the throttle valve regulates the petrol-to-air ratio between one-eighth and one-quarter throttle. The needle jet (14) and the jet needle (23) take over the mixture regulation between one-quarter and three-quarter throttle, and the mixture strength is determined by the relative position of the needle in the clip (4) attached to the throttle valve (24). When the throttle is opened beyond three-quarters, the mixture strength is determined only by the size of the main jet. Note that the main jet (16) does not spray petrol direct into the carburettor mixing chamber, but discharges through the needle jet into the primary air chamber. From there it enters the main choke through the primary air choke. The latter has a two-way compensating action in conjunction with the "bleed" holes in the needle jet. Pilot and main jet behaviour are not affected by this two-way compensation which governs only acceleration at normal cruising speed.

TUNING THE CARBURETTOR

Normally it is unwise to interfere with the maker's carburettor setting (*see* Table I) unless there is a very special reason for doing so. However, it is sometimes desirable to make a slow-running adjustment with the pilot air-adjusting screw.

To obtain good slow-running, observe the following instructions—

To vary the strength of the normal running mixture, it is necessary to adjust the height of the needle in the throttle valve, or else to fit a larger or smaller size main jet. The condition of the sparking plug provides an excellent guide to the condition of the mixture.

Altering Slow-running Adjustment. This should be effected with the engine already warmed up, the throttle twist-grip closed and the throttle slide abutting the throttle-stop screw. The air lever should be fully open and the ignition lever (where automatic ignition-advance is not provided) should be set to obtain the best slow-running (half to two-thirds advanced).

TABLE I

AMAL ("MONOBLOC") CARBURETTOR SETTINGS FOR 1955-66

B.S.A. Model	Main Jet Size	Pilot Jet Size	Throttle Valve	Needle Position
B31, B32 (air filter) . .	200	30	376/3½	2
B31, B32 (no filter) . .	260	30	376/3½	2
B33, B34 (air filter) . .	210	25	376/3½	3
B33, B34 (no filter) . .	260	25	376/3¼	3
M33 (1955-8) . . .	260	25	376/3¼	3
B40 (1961-5) . . .	190	20	376/3	3
B40 SS90 (1962-6) . .	200	30	389/3½	3

First *screw in* the pilot-air adjusting screw until the mixture is excessively rich and the engine commences to run unevenly. Now weaken the mixture by *unscrewing* the pilot-air adjusting screw until the engine runs evenly. Avoid excessive weakening of the mixture which would probably cause the engine to spit back through the carburettor or even stop when the throttle is opened. With the pilot-air adjusting screw properly set, it may be found that the engine is running excessively fast. In this case unscrew the throttle-stop until the engine runs at an even and steady tick-over.

Where a considerable throttle-stop adjustment has to be made, further adjustment of the pilot-air adjusting screw may be required in order to obtain a perfect slow-running mixture. Avoid an excessively slow tick-over, as this is apt to induce low-temperature condensation on the cylinder walls and cause variable starting under variable atmospheric conditions.

It is important to avoid excessive richness of the slow-running mixture, especially if much riding is done on small throttle openings; if the mixture is too rich, considerable running on the pilot jet will occur *while riding*, with consequently a high fuel consumption.

Aim at obtaining the best tick-over on a mixture bordering on the weak side. The engine should be quite near the point of spitting-back. Rev the engine up and down sharply several times and note whether the exhaust is nice and crisp, with no "flat spots" as the twist-grip is rotated. It is essential to obtain good acceleration as well as good tick-over. When making this test, the ignition lever (where fitted) must be *fully advanced*. Never run the engine fast with the ignition lever even slightly retarded.

Altering Jet-needle Position. The tapered jet needle secured by a clip to the throttle valve regulates the mixture between about *one-quarter and three-quarter full throttle*. The tapered jet needle and the needle jet gradually wear, through continuous movement of the throttle, and this slowly enriches the mixture within the throttle range just referred to, thereby increasing the petrol consumption. The remedy is to lower the tapered jet needle *one notch* by securing it in No. 2 position or, in the event of bad wear existing, in No. 1 position (top groove). If an excessively rich mixture persists after lowering the jet needle so that it is in the top notch, renew both the jet needle and the needle jet. The size of the main jet (below the needle jet) determines the mixture strength from *three-quarter to full throttle*.

Poor Slow-running. If it is found impossible to obtain good slow-running by making the pilot air adjustment as described on page 13, it is possible that there are air leaks, due to a poor joint at the carburettor attachment to the cylinder and/or a worn inlet-valve guide. Badly seating valves will also weaken the mixture. Defects in the ignition system may also be responsible for poor tick-over. The sparking plug may be oily, or the points set too close (*see* page 56). Possibly the spark is excessively advanced or the contact-breaker needs attention (*see* page 61). See that the H.T. pick-up brush on "Magdyno" models is bedding down and in good condition; also that the slip-ring is clean. Examine the H.T. cable for signs of shorting.

Obstructed Pilot-jet. If the pilot-jet adjustment does not obtain the desired results and the engine will not idle nicely with the throttle almost closed, the air lever wide open, and the ignition (if manual control is provided) half to two-thirds advanced, it is possible that the pilot jet is obstructed. The jet on the former standard type carburettor is actually a duct drilled in the jet block, is very small, and can readily become choked. On the "Monobloc" type carburettor it is only necessary to remove the cover nut below the pilot jet (17) shown in Fig. 5, and unscrew the pilot jet. Clear the jet by blowing through it, also the main jet if necessary.

HINTS ON MAINTENANCE

To Dismantle "Monobloc" Type Carburettor. Close the two-level petrol tap and disconnect the petrol pipe by undoing the banjo bolt (8) over the float chamber (*see* Fig. 5). Referring to Fig. 5, unscrew the mixing-chamber knurled cap-ring (2) on top of the carburettor and also remove the two nuts securing the carburettor flange to the face of the inlet port. Then remove the body of the carburettor (21), complete with the integral float chamber (13). While removing the carburettor, pull the air valve (3), and the throttle valve (24) from the mixing chamber and tie them up temporarily out of the way. As mentioned in the instructions for the standard type carburettor, it is rarely necessary to disconnect the slides from the cables. Check that the flange washer is sound.

Further dismantling is straightforward. Referring to Fig. 5, to remove the jet needle (23), withdraw the jet-needle clip (4) on top of the throttle valve, and remove the needle. To obtain access to the float (10), remove the three screws (11) securing the float-chamber cover (12). Lift out the hinged float (10) and withdraw the moulded-nylon needle (9). Lay both aside for cleaning. The float-chamber vent, by the way, is embodied in the tickler assembly (7), and the top-feed union houses a filter element of fine gauze which is readily accessible for cleaning.

To remove the main jet (16), remove the main-jet cover and unscrew the jet from the jet holder (15), which should also be unscrewed. Remove the jet-block locating screw (19) to the left of and slightly below the pilot air-adjusting screw. Then push or tap out the jet block (5) and fibre seal (22) through the large end of the mixing chamber (21). To remove the pilot jet (17), remove the pilot-jet cover nut and unscrew the jet.

Cleaning the Carburettor. Wash all the carburettor components thoroughly clean with petrol and blow through the various ducts and passages to make sure that they are quite clear. Avoid using a fluffy rag for drying purposes. Pay special attention to the small pilot-jet passages in the jet block. See that all impurities are removed from inside the float chamber. Do not forget to clean the detachable pilot jet and the filter gauze inside the top-feed union for the float chamber.

Inspecting Components. When dismantling the carburettor it is advisable to make a close inspection of the various parts if the carburettor has been in continuous service for a considerable period.

1. *The Float Chamber.* Examine the components very carefully and check that the vent is unobstructed. The float must be in perfect condition. Check that it does not leak by shaking it. Never try and repair a damaged float, but always fit a new one. Clean the moulded-nylon float needle thoroughly and check it for efficient action. Examine the joint faces of the float chamber and float-chamber cover for any bruising or damage which would prevent the joint being petrol-tight after assembly.

2. *The Throttle Valve.* Test this for good fit and no slackness in the mixing chamber. Look for excessive scoring on the front side and excessive wear on its rear face. If close inspection reveals excessive wear, renew the slide and when doing this make quite sure that the new slide has the correct degree of cut-away (*see* page 13).

3. *The Air Valve.* Inspect this also for excessive wear and make sure there is no slackness. Verify the proper fit of the slide in the jet block. Check that the return springs for the throttle valve and the air valve are in perfect condition and have not lost their compressive strength.

4. *The Jet-needle Clip.* The spring clip securing the tapered needle to the throttle valve must grip the needle firmly, and free rotation must *not* occur, as this causes the needle groove to wear. Always be careful to replace the needle with the clip in the correct groove (*see* page 13).

5. *The Needle-jet.* Look for wear and possible scoring of its orifice

which usually occurs after covering about 15,000 miles. The movement of the stainless-steel jet needle is ultimately bound to cause some wear.

6. *The Jet Block.* Before tapping this home in the mixing chamber verify by blowing that the pilot air duct is clear and that the jet-block fibre seal is in good condition.

7. *The Carburettor Flange.* Examine this for truth with a straight-edge. Distortion sometimes occurs, and this may cause an air leak. If the flange face is slightly concave, file and rub down the face with emery cloth laid on a surface plate until it is dead flat and smooth. Alternatively have it faced on a machine. Renew the rubber "O" ring (where fitted) unless perfect and see that the joint washer is in sound condition.

Assembling "Monobloc" Type Carburettor. Do this in the reverse order of dismantling. Referring to Fig. 5, screw home the pilot jet (17) and the pilot-jet cover nut, not omitting to replace its washer. Push or tap home the jet block (5) and fibre seal (22) through the large end of the mixing chamber (21). Check that the fibre-seal fitted to the stub of the jet block is in good condition. Then fit the jet-block locating-screw (19). Screw the main-jet holder (15) into the jet block, after checking that the washer for the holder is sound. Next screw the main jet (16) into the main-jet holder.

Replace the moulded-nylon needle (9) in the float chamber (13), and fit the hinged float (10) with the *narrow* side of the hinge uppermost. Afterwards fit the float-chamber cover (12) and secure by means of the three screws (11). Verify that the cover and body faces are undamaged and quite clean. Renew the washer.

If previously removed, attach the jet needle (23) to the throttle valve (24) and secure with the jet-needle clip (4), making sure that the clip enters the correct groove (*see* Table I on page 13).

Position the carburettor-flange washer, and offer up the carburettor to the face of the inlet port after easing the air and throttle valves (3) and (24) down into the mixing chamber. When easing the throttle valve home, make sure that the tapered jet needle (23) really enters the hole in the jet block (5). Secure the carburettor flange firmly to the engine by means of the two nuts, and tighten these evenly. Tighten down firmly the mixing-chamber knurled cap-ring (2) and see that the throttle slide works freely when this is tightened down

Finally reconnect the petrol pipe by tightening the banjo securing-bolt (8) over the float chamber (13).

The C. & W. Air Filter (B31–B34, M33 Models). This filter is of the "oil-dip" type and the filter element requires to be removed about every 5,000 miles (in the U.K.) for cleaning and dipping in suitable oil. The filter element should be renewed after a big mileage when cleaning no longer frees embedded dirt, or spots of light are visible through the element on holding it up to the light. The filter assembly is mounted in front of the battery carrier and is connected to the air-intake stub of the Amal "Monobloc" carburettor by a short rubber sleeve.

To remove the filter element, first free the air-filter cover by removing the two securing-bolts which pass through elongated slots; the lower bolt secures the cover to the frame member below the saddle; the other one attaches the cover to the battery clamping-strap. Disconnect the rubber sleeve connecting the air-filter cover to the air-intake stub of the

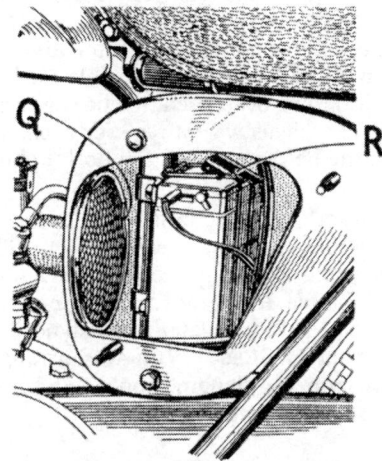

FIG. 6. AIR FILTER AND BATTERY BOX (MODELS B40, B40 SS90)

Q. Air filter circlip   R. Clasp for battery

carburettor; slip the sleeve off the cover and leave the other end undisturbed. Withdraw the cover and then remove the filter element from it after prising out the wire circlip with a screwdriver.

Wash the filter element very thoroughly in petrol, dry it, and then submerge it completely in thin oil (about SAE 20) for a few minutes. Remove the element, allow all surplus oil to drain off, and afterwards secure the element to the air-filter cover by means of the circlip. Then replace the cover on the machine. attaching it to the frame member below the saddle and to the battery strap by means of the two securing-screws. Finally reconnect the rubber sleeve to the filter cover.

The Air Filter on Models B40, B40 SS90. The air filter is located as shown in Fig. 6. About every 1,000 miles remove the cover from the air filter and battery box. It is secured by two screws. Prise out the wire circlip (Q) and remove the perforated cover and filter element. Wash the element in petrol and dry thoroughly.

CHAPTER III

CARE OF THE LIGHTING SYSTEM

LUCAS electric lighting equipment has been specified on all 1955 B.S.A. models onwards. Up to and including 1957 a Lucas "Magdyno" was used for lighting and ignition, the dynamo being fitted above the magneto. The dynamo charges the battery which is responsible for lighting only. From 1958 onward coil ignition has been used, a Lucas alternator being housed in the oil-bath chain case. This with a rectifier keeps the battery charged and the current from the battery is used for both lighting and ignition.

The Lucas "Magdyno." This consists of a magneto and a 6-volt dynamo strapped together to form a single unit. The dynamo can if necessary be detached and the magneto half only used. In this case a protective cover (obtainable from the makers) must be fitted over the gears to exclude dirt. All 1955 and later "Magdynos" and dynamos have compensated-voltage-control fitted. With this arrangement the cut-out is mounted separately from the dynamo, only two brushes are fitted, and charging is entirely automatic (*see* page 20).

DYNAMO MAINTENANCE (1955-7)

When removing the metal cover-band, it is not necessary to disconnect the negative lead of the battery at the battery end, but always disconnect the battery lead when making any required adjustments to the wiring circuit. To disconnect, push back the rubber shield and unscrew the cable connector, being careful not to touch the frame with the cable and cause a short circuit. When reconnecting, make sure the rubber shield is pulled well over the connector. Disconnect at terminals (screw type).

If at any time the motor-cycle is ridden with the battery disconnected, or in any way out of service, it is possible to run with the switch in any position without causing damage to the electrical equipment.

The Commutator Brushes. Every 10,000 miles remove the dynamo cover (the metal cover-band) and inspect the brushgear and commutator. It is very important to make sure that the brushes move freely in their holders. This can be easily ascertained by holding back each retaining spring and gently pulling each flexible lead, when the brush should move without sluggishness. It should also return to its original position directly the lead is released. When testing a brush in this way, release it gently and see that the spring is clear of the brush holder, otherwise the brush may get chipped. The brushes should be clean and "bed" over the whole surface; that is, the face in contact with the commutator should appear uniformly polished. Dirty or sticking brushes may be cleaned, after removal, with a cloth moistened with petrol. See that they are replaced in their original positions.

If the brushes become so badly worn that it is necessary to remove them, this can easily be done as follows: release the eyelet on the brush lead by unscrewing the hexagonal nut or screw at the terminal; then, holding

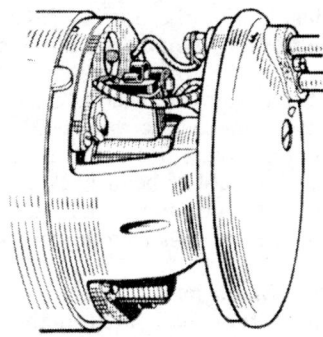

FIG. 7. COMMUTATOR END OF LUCAS E3L DYNAMO

Some thin machine oil should be put in the lubricator about every 2,000–3,000 miles.
The driving-end bearing is packed with H.M.P. grease on assembly.

back the spring lever out of the way, withdraw the brush from its holder. Renew with genuine Lucas brushes.

The brush springs should be inspected occasionally to see that they have sufficient tension to keep the brushes firmly pressed against the commutator when the machine is running. It is particularly necessary to keep this in mind when the brushes have been in use a long time and are very much worn down. Owners are cautioned that it is unwise to insert brushes of a grade other than that supplied with the dynamo, or to change the tension springs. The arrangement provided has been made only after many years' experience, and will be found to give the best results and the longest life. When the brushes become so worn that they no longer "bed down" on the commutator, new brushes should be fitted by a Lucas service depot; this will ensure that the brushes are properly "bedded."

The Commutator must be Clean. The surface of the commutator segments should be kept clean and free from oil or brush dust, etc. Should any grease or oil work its way on to the commutator through over-lubrication, not only will it cause sparking but, in addition, carbon and copper dust will collect in the grooves between the commutator segments.

The best way to clean the commutator, without disconnecting any leads, is to remove from its box-holder one of the main brushes and, inserting a dry duster, hold it by means of a piece of wood against the commutator surface, at the same time causing the armature to be rotated. If very dirty, moisten the duster with petrol. If the commutator has been neglected for a long period, it may need cleaning with fine glasspaper, which is more difficult to do. The segments should be *dark bronze* and highly polished.

Lubrication of the Dynamo. *See* Fig. 7.

The Dynamo Terminals. On the Lucas "Magdyno" with separate voltage-control unit the positive dynamo terminal is marked "D" and the shunt-field terminal "F" on the cover. To connect up, first slacken the fixing screw on the terminal block and remove the clamping plate. Then withdraw the metal sleeve from each terminal. The cables should then be passed through the clamping plate holes and bared at the ends for $\frac{3}{8}$ in. Now fit the sleeves over the cables, bend back the wires over them and push the sleeves home into the terminals, finally screwing down the clamping plate. *Note: yellow sleeving goes to terminal "D."*

To Remove Dynamo ("Magdyno" Models). Loosen the "Magdyno" securing-strap and remove the small nut (on the off side) securing the dynamo to the top of the gear housing.

Compensated Voltage Control. This is used for all Lucas dynamos. Wiring diagrams: *see* pages 30-31. The control unit (Model MCR1) comprises the cut-out and voltage control (working on the trembler principle) neatly housed in a box on the rear mudguard, or in the tool box on "swinging arm" models. It keeps the battery properly charged automatically, the dynamo output varying according to the state of charge of the battery and the load.

With C.V.C. equipment the lighting switch is provided with only three positions—"Off," "L," and "H" (*see* page 27). In all three positions the dynamo gives a controlled output, thus relieving the rider of much responsibility. The regulator begins to operate when the dynamo voltage reaches about 7.3 volts. During daylight running when the battery is well charged the ammeter may indicate a charge of only 1 or 2 amp, for the dynamo gives only a trickle charge.

The regulator provides for an increase of dynamo output as soon as the lamps are switched on. The effect of switching the lamps on after a long run with the battery voltage high is often to cause a temporary discharge reading at the ammeter, but fairly soon the voltage falls and the regulator responds, thereby causing the output of the dynamo to balance the load of the lamps.

When the battery is in a discharged state, the regulator increases the dynamo output and restores the battery to its normal state of charge in the shortest possible time.

Do Not Tamper with the C.V.C. Unit. The unit is sealed by the makers, and does not need adjustment once it is correctly set. The only conceivable trouble is from the contacts oxidizing or welding together, owing to accidental crossing of the dynamo field and positive leads. Be careful if making wiring alterations (*see* page 29). Referring to Fig. 8, make sure that the C.V.C. unit connexions are correct, tight, and that the insulation is sound.

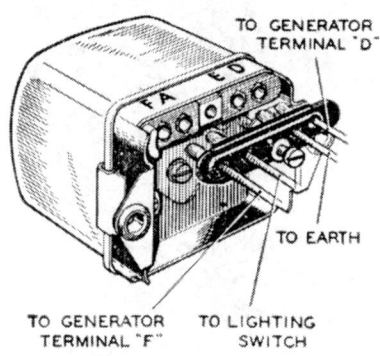

TO GENERATOR
TERMINAL 'D'

TO EARTH

TO GENERATOR
TERMINAL 'F'

TO LIGHTING
SWITCH

FIG. 8. LUCAS CUT-OUT AND
REGULATOR UNIT CONNEXIONS

Should you fit a "Lucas-Nife" battery in place of the lead-acid type, you must fit a new regulator to ensure a good charging rate with a discharged battery. You are advised to have the changeover made at a Lucas service depot and to visit a depot whenever any serious electrical fault develops.

Absence of Fuses. In order to simplify the system as far as possible, no fuse is provided. If all the connexions are kept clean and tight, there is no possibility of any excess current.

Ammeter. This gives a reading of the amount of current flowing into or from the battery and shows whether the equipment is functioning satisfactorily. It is of the centre-zero type and mounted as shown in Figs. 1–3.

THE ALTERNATOR AND RECTIFIER (1958–66)

The Lucas Alternator. On all 1958–66 B.S.A. models there is no dynamo, a Lucas 60-watt alternator being fitted. As may be observed in Fig. 9, the stator of the alternator is mounted on three distance pillars projecting from the crankcase casting. The rotor is attached to the engine shaft, the engine-shaft shock-absorber hitherto fitted being omitted.

Because the alternator unit has no rotating windings, commutator. brushgear, or oil seals, no maintenance whatever is called for other than to see that the three snap-connectors in the output cables are tight and clean, and the leads unfrayed. If it should be necessary for any reason to remove the rotor, note that keepers need not be fitted to the rotor poles.

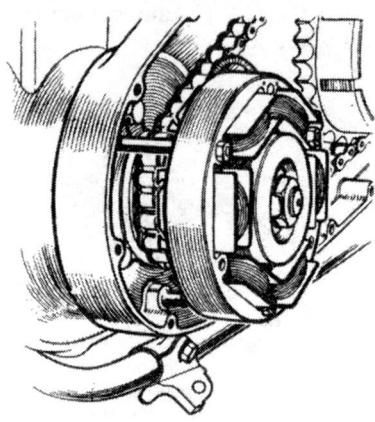

FIG 9. THE LUCAS ALTERNATOR UNIT HOUSED INSIDE THE OIL-BATH CHAIN CASE ON THE 1958–66 MODELS

(By courtesy of "Motor Cycle.")

The Lucas Rectifier. Electrical connexion is made between the coils of the six-coil stator and a full-wave rectifier clamped to the motor-cycle frame. The rectifier consists of four plates (coated on one side with silenium) and operates like a non-return valve, allowing current to pass in one direction only. The alternating current from the alternator is thus converted into uni-directional (d.c.) current for charging the battery. The only rectifier maintenance necessary is to keep the connexions tight and clean, and occasion-ally to check that the nut securing the rectifier unit is absolutely tight. The nut which clamps the rectifier plates together must under no circum-stances be slackened.

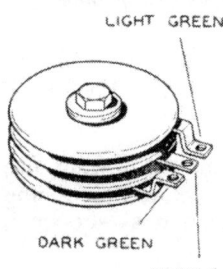

LIGHT GREEN

DARK GREEN

PURPLE

FIG. 10. THE LUCAS RECTIFIER CONNEXIONS

Should it be necessary for any reason to dis-connect the leads from the rectifier, they must be reconnected correctly as indicated in Fig. 10.

CARE OF THE BATTERY (LEAD-ACID TYPE)

It is of the utmost importance that the battery should receive regular attention to keep it in good condition.

The following are the most important maintenance hints for a Lucas battery—

1. Keep the electrolyte level correct.
2. Add only distilled water, never tap water.
3. Test the condition of the battery by taking occasional readings of the specific gravity of the acid with a hydrometer.
4. Never leave the battery in a badly discharged condition.

FIG. 11. BATTERY LOCATION ON 1955–60 "SWINGING ARM" MODELS

Battery Removal. Removal of the battery is desirable before topping-up its cells.

On 1955–60 "swinging arm" models the battery is mounted beneath the dual seat (*see* Fig. 11). To remove the battery, first remove the two bolts from under the rear of the dual seat and withdraw the dual seat backwards from the forward locating bar. Then remove the two small bolts securing the battery strap, disconnect the battery terminals, and lift the battery out.

On the 1961–6 Models B40, B40 SS90 the battery is mounted in a special compartment beneath the dualseat. Referring to Fig. 6, lift the clasp (*R*) and withdraw the battery from its carrier. The battery lead connexions must, of course, first be disconnected.

Topping-up the Cells. Examine the acid level about every two weeks (weekly: B40, B40 SS90), and even more frequently in tropical climates.

Take off the battery lid; remove the vent plugs. Inspect the hole in each vent plug and make certain that it is not obstructed. A choked vent plug hole will result in an increase of pressure in the cell owing to "gassing," and this may cause trouble.

Wipe the top of the battery clean with a rag and also verify that the rubber washer often fitted beneath each vent plug, to prevent leakage, is in position. After wiping the top of the battery, either destroy the rag or wash it thoroughly, using several changes of water. See that a supply of clean distilled water is to hand.*

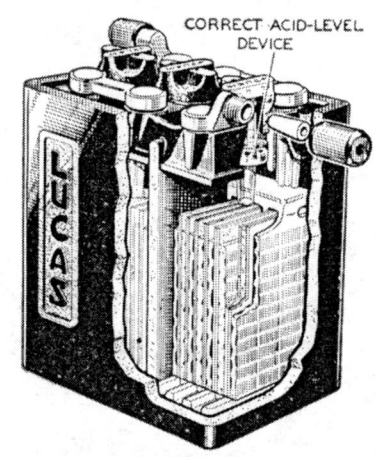

FIG. 12. LUCAS BATTERY AS FITTED TO 1955–60 MODELS

Be careful not to hold a naked light near the vents. If the level is below the tops of the separators, add *distilled* water as required to bring the level correct. This should be done just *before* a charge run, as the agitation due to running and the gassing will thoroughly mix the solution.

To top-up a Lucas battery of 1955–60 type having an acid-level device, pour distilled water round its flange (not down the tube) until no more drains through into the cell. This occurs when the level of the electrolyte reaches the bottom of the central tube and prevents further escape of air displaced by the topping-up water. Lift the tube slightly to permit the small quantity of water in the flange to drain into the cell; the level of the electrolyte will then be correct. With the Lucas battery fitted to a 1961–6 Model B40 or B40 SS90 add distilled water until it reaches the blue line on the outside of the battery (*see* Fig. 13).

* The distilled water, unlike the sulphuric acid, is lost gradually by evaporation. It is obtainable from garages and chemists.

Do not add acid to the electrolyte unless some of the solution has been accidentally spilled. In this case add diluted sulphuric acid of specific gravity equal to that in the cells. Finally replace the vent plugs, fit the battery, and fasten it securely. See that the battery leads are firmly and correctly reconnected.

Replenishing a Lucas Battery Filler. When replenishing a Lucas battery filler with distilled water, see that the screw-on nozzle is replaced correctly. Be sure that the rubber washer is fitted over the valve with the

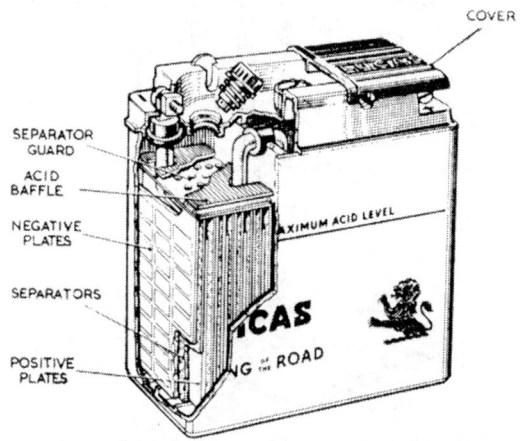

FIG. 13. LUCAS BATTERY FITTED TO 1961–6 MODELS B40, B40 SS90
A blue line indicates the maximum acid level

small peg in the centre of the valve engaging the hole in the projecting boss of the washer.

Checking Specific Gravity. Motor-cyclists seldom bother about this procedure, but checking the S.G. readings of the electrolyte is desirable by yourself or at a garage if some loss of acid is known to have occurred, or if the general condition of the battery is suspect. Fig. 14 shows the correct method of using a Lucas hydrometer to check the S.G. reading of the electrolyte in each cell. S.G. readings should not be taken immediately after topping-up the battery, as the electrolyte will not then be thoroughly mixed.

After a sample has been taken and checked, it must, of course, be returned to the cell. The taking of S.G. readings with a hydrometer is the most efficient way of ascertaining the state of charge of the battery. The S.G. readings should be approximately the *same for all three cells*. Should the reading for one cell differ substantially from the readings for the others, probably some acid has been spilled or has leaked from the cell concerned. There is also a possibility of a short-circuit between the battery plates. In the latter case it will be necessary to return the battery to a Lucas service depot for attention.

Under no circumstances must the battery be permitted to remain in a discharged condition for long, or serious deterioration will occur. A

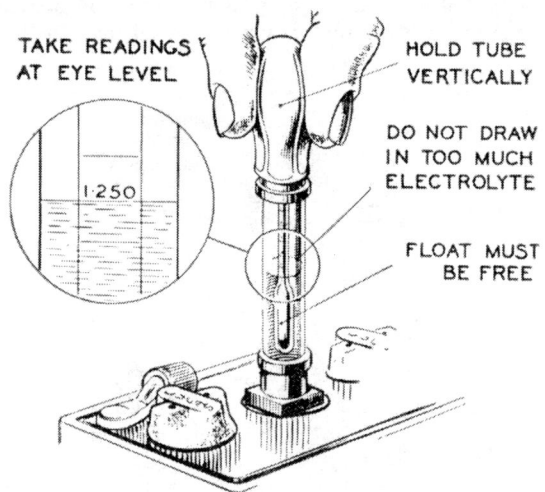

TAKE READINGS
AT EYE LEVEL

HOLD TUBE
VERTICALLY

DO NOT DRAW
IN TOO MUCH
ELECTROLYTE

1·250

FLOAT MUST
BE FREE

FIG. 14. LUCAS HYDROMETER BEING USED TO CHECK SPECIFIC GRAVITY
OF BATTERY ELECTROLYTE

low state of charge is often caused through parking the machine for long periods with the lighting switch in the "L" position, unaccompanied by much daylight running. After checking the S.G. readings wipe the top of the battery and remove any spilled electrolyte; replace the three vent plugs and the battery lid.

TABLE II

SPECIFIC GRAVITY READINGS FOR LUCAS BATTERIES

Temperature	Fully Charged	Requires Charging
80° F	1·285	1·235
60° F	1·295	1·245

Battery Connexions. Always keep the battery connexions clean, free from corrosion, and tight; otherwise the ammeter readings will *not* indicate the true state of charge of the battery. To prevent corrosion they should be smeared with petroleum jelly.

Storage. If the equipment is laid by for several months, the battery must be given a small charge from a separate source of electrical energy about once a month, in order to prevent any permanent sulphation of the plates. In no circumstances must the electrolyte be removed.

LUCAS LAMPS

Lucas Lighting Switch Positions. Automatic-voltage-control is provided on all 1955 and later B.S.A. models, and therefore the dynamo or alternator charges the battery when the engine is running with the lighting switch in any of its three positions which are as follows—

(1) Headlamp, tail lamp, speedometer, and sidecar lamp (where fitted) switched off.

(2) Headlamp pilot bulb, tail lamp, speedometer, and sidecar lamp (where fitted) on.

(3) Headlamp main bulb, tail lamp, speedometer, and sidecar lamp (where fitted) on. Main beam controlled by separate dipper switch.

Adjusting the Headlamp Position. If the headlamp is incorrectly aligned maximum road illumination will not be obtained, and other road users may be inconvenienced by dazzle. It is easy to rectify both faults.

The best method of checking the alignment of the headlamp is to stand your B.S.A. facing a light-coloured wall at a distance of approximately 25–30 feet. Switch on the main driving light and note if the beam is projected straight ahead and parallel with the ground.

Take vertical measurements from the centre of the headlamp, and from the centre of the illuminated circle on the wall to the ground. Both measurements should be equal. If they are unequal, loosen the two fixing bolts securing the headlamp in the front-fork mounting brackets (where fitted) and tilt the headlamp until the centre of the beam is truly parallel with the ground. Afterwards tighten the two headlamp fixing bolts firmly. On some recent models such as Models B40, B40 SS90 slacken the three screws securing the headlamp fixing rim and move the lamp until the beam is aligned correctly. Note that many garages now have a Lucas beam setter.

Correct Focusing. On all new B.S.A.s the double-filament main bulb is carefully focused to give the best illumination. Provided that Lucas bulbs of the correct wattage and number are fitted as replacements,

focusing is bound to be correct. All 1955–66 models have a Lucas head-lamp with a main bulb which is permanently "pre-focused."
For correct bulb renewals, *see* below.

Cleaning Lucas Lamps. The reflector is most important. Never scratch its surface during handling, and avoid finger-marking the surface.

Clean the black surfaces of the lamp body with a good car polish, and polish the chromium-plated rim with a chamois leather or a soft, dry cloth, after first washing off any dirt with water.

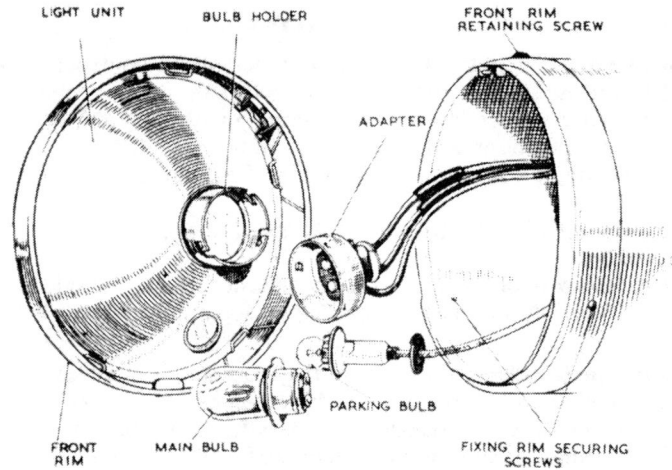

FIG. 15. TYPICAL LUCAS HEADLAMP WITH LIGHT-UNIT ASSEMBLY AND
"PRE-FOCUS" MAIN BULB
The reflector is sealed to the glass. The parking bulb is a push fit in the reflector.

BULB RENEWAL

When fitting a new bulb to a Lucas headlamp, see that the new bulb is of Lucas manufacture. Lucas bulbs are specially designed for use with Lucas reflectors; another make of bulb may *not* always give the best results.

Non-focusing Type Headlamps. To obtain access to the bulbs on all 1955–66 headlamps of the sealed-unit type and provided with a "pre-focus" main bulb, remove the headlamp rim, complete with light unit assembly (*see* Fig. 15); to do this loosen the screw on top of the headlamp shell and pull the rim away at the top.

The Lucas "pre-focus" bulb (No. 312) has a broad locating flange; it can be fitted in the bulb holder in one position only, a notch on the flange engaging a projection inside the bulb holder. The adaptor which secures the "pre-focus" bulb comprises a bayonet-fitting cap, and this also can be fitted in one position only, its prongs not being symmetrical.

Referring to Fig. 15, to replace a "pre-focus" main bulb, press the adaptor inwards, turn it *anti-clockwise*, pull it off, and remove the bulb from the holder in the rear of the reflector. Fit the new bulb in the holder, engage the projections on the inside of the adaptor with the slots in the bulb holder, press on the adaptor, and secure it by turning *clockwise*.

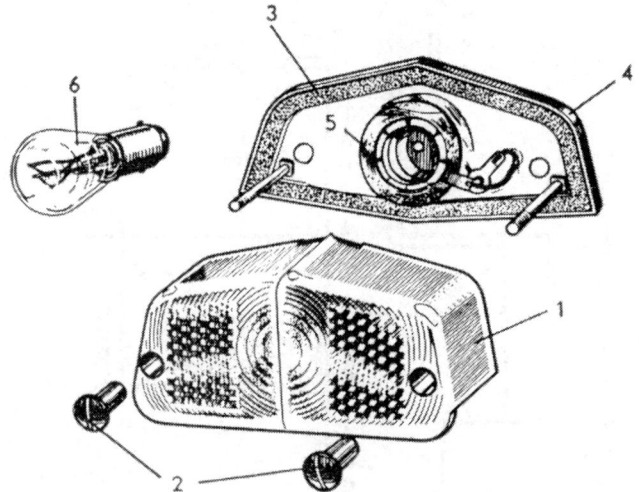

FIG. 16. THE LUCAS 564 STOP-TAIL LAMP (1960 ONWARDS)

1. Lens and window	4. Base assembly
2. Nut	5. Grummet
3. Gasket	6. Bulb

Bulbs for 1955–66 Lamps. For all 1955–66 models with a headlamp having a "pre-focus" main bulb, the correct bulb renewals are as follows—

Main bulb: 6-volt, 30/24-watt, double-filament, Lucas No. 312.
Pilot bulb: 6-volt, 3-watt, Lucas No. 988.
Tail lamp bulb: 6-volt, 6-watt, Lucas No. 205.
Stop-tail lamp bulb (where fitted): 6-volt, 18/6-watt, Lucas No. 384.

WIRING OF THE EQUIPMENT

Before making any alteration to the wiring, or removing the lighting switch from the back of the Lucas headlamp, disconnect the negative lead at the battery to prevent the possibility of short circuits. For wiring see Figs. 17–20.

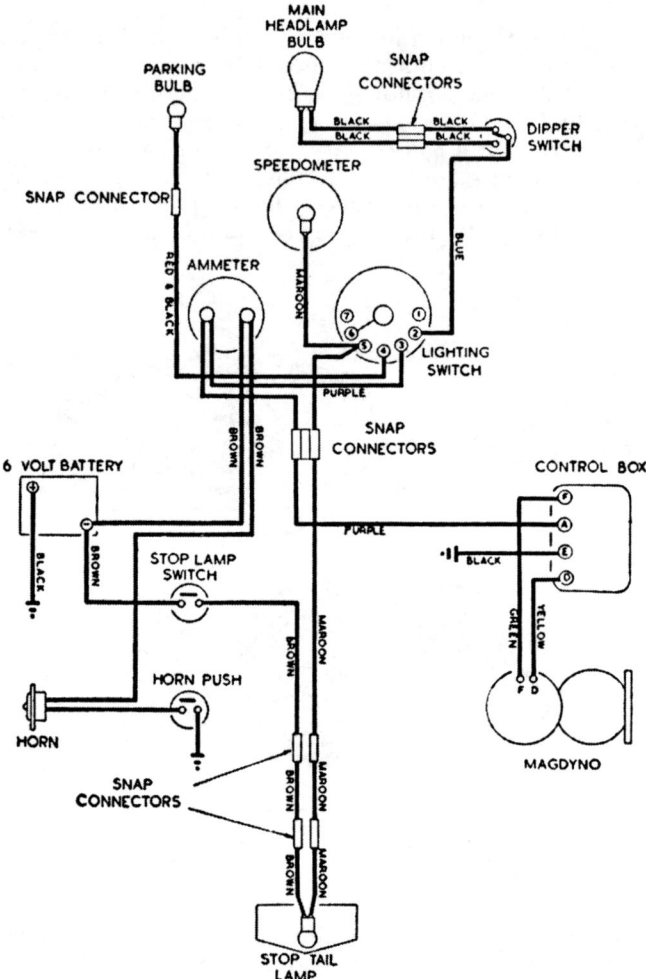

FIG. 17. WIRING DIAGRAM FOR LUCAS "MAGDYNO" LIGHTING EQUIPMENT
WITH COMPENSATED VOLTAGE CONTROL (1955 "SWINGING ARM"
MODELS)

This (positive earth) diagram applies to 1955 "B" models with SS700P headlamp and
cowl embodying the ammeter, lighting switch, and speedometer. It also applies to
1955 models with plunger-type rear suspension, but in this instance the horn is
connected to the negative terminal of the battery.

(B.S.A. Motor Cycles, Ltd.)

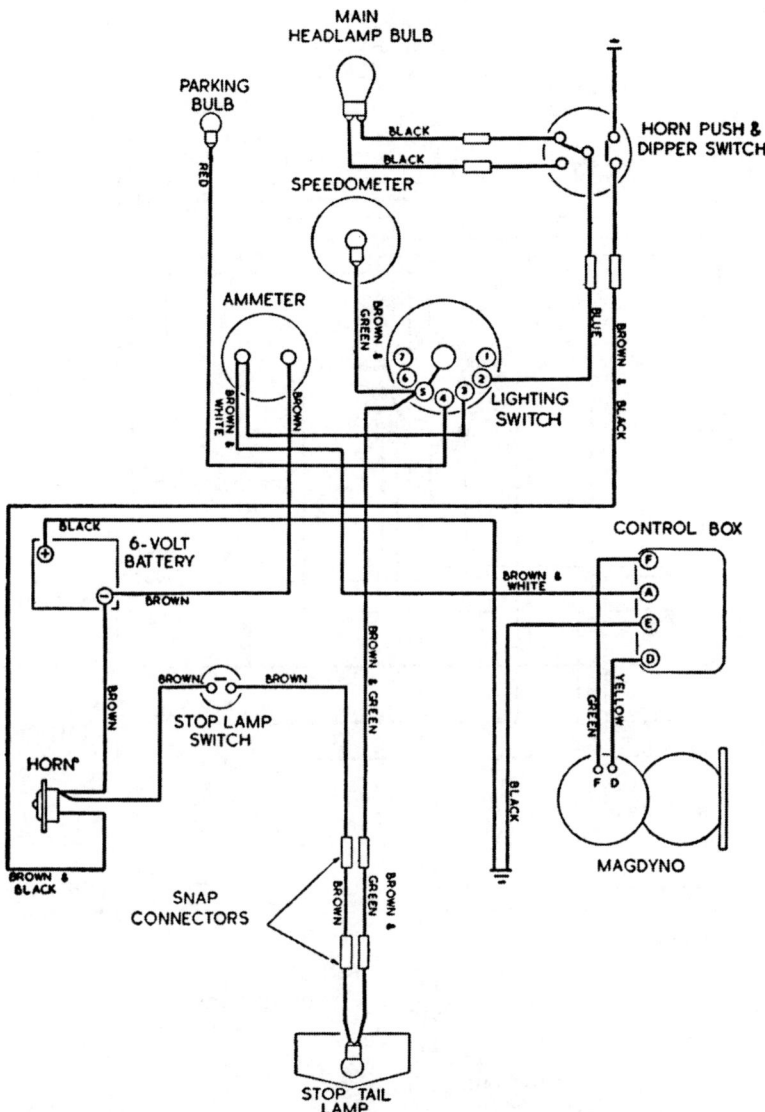

FIG. 18. WIRING DIAGRAM FOR LUCAS "MAGDYNO" LIGHTING EQUIPMENT
WITH COMPENSATED VOLTAGE CONTROL (1956–7 O.H.V. MODELS)

This (positive earth) diagram applies to machines with cowled SS700P headlamp
and combined horn and dipper switch. Note that on the "swinging arm" O.H.V.
models the horn lead is connected to the ammeter as shown in Fig. 17.

(*B.S.A. Motor Cycles, Ltd.*)

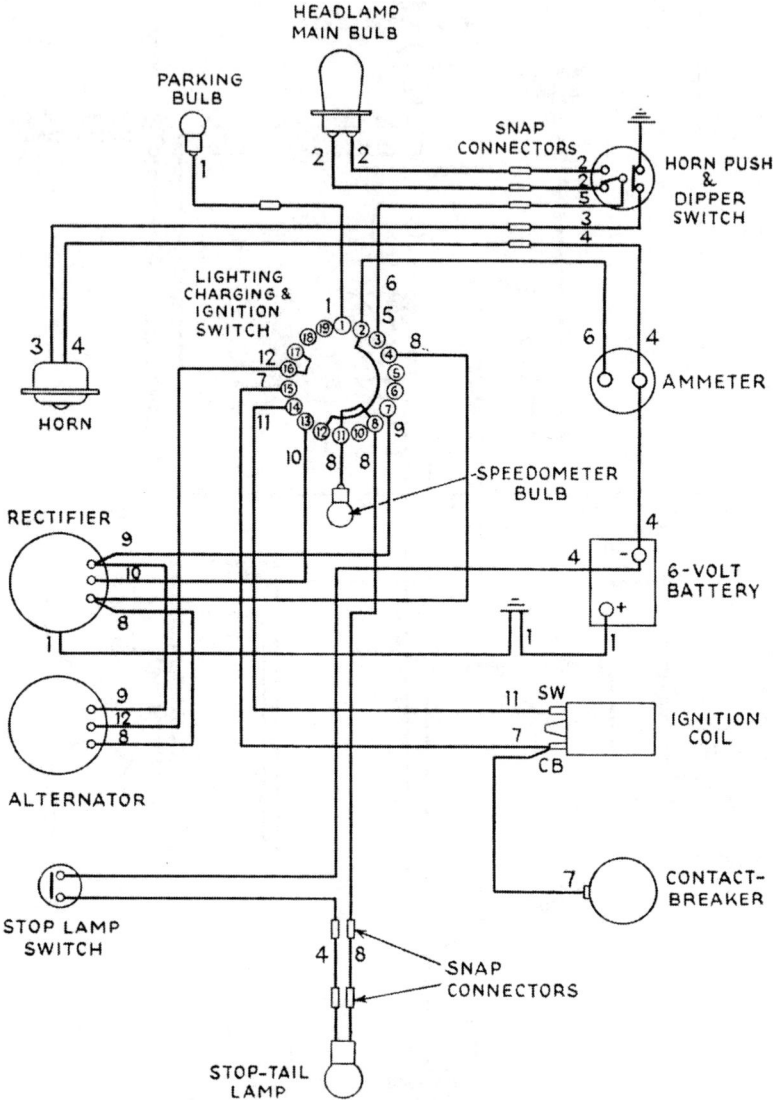

FIG. 19. WIRING DIAGRAM FOR LUCAS ALTERNATOR AND RECTIFIER
EQUIPMENT

This (positive earth) diagram applies to all 1958–60 O.H.V. "swinging arm" models.
There is, of course, no dynamo or C.V.C. unit. For key to sleeve colours, *see* page 34.

(*B.S.A. Motor Cycles, Ltd.*)

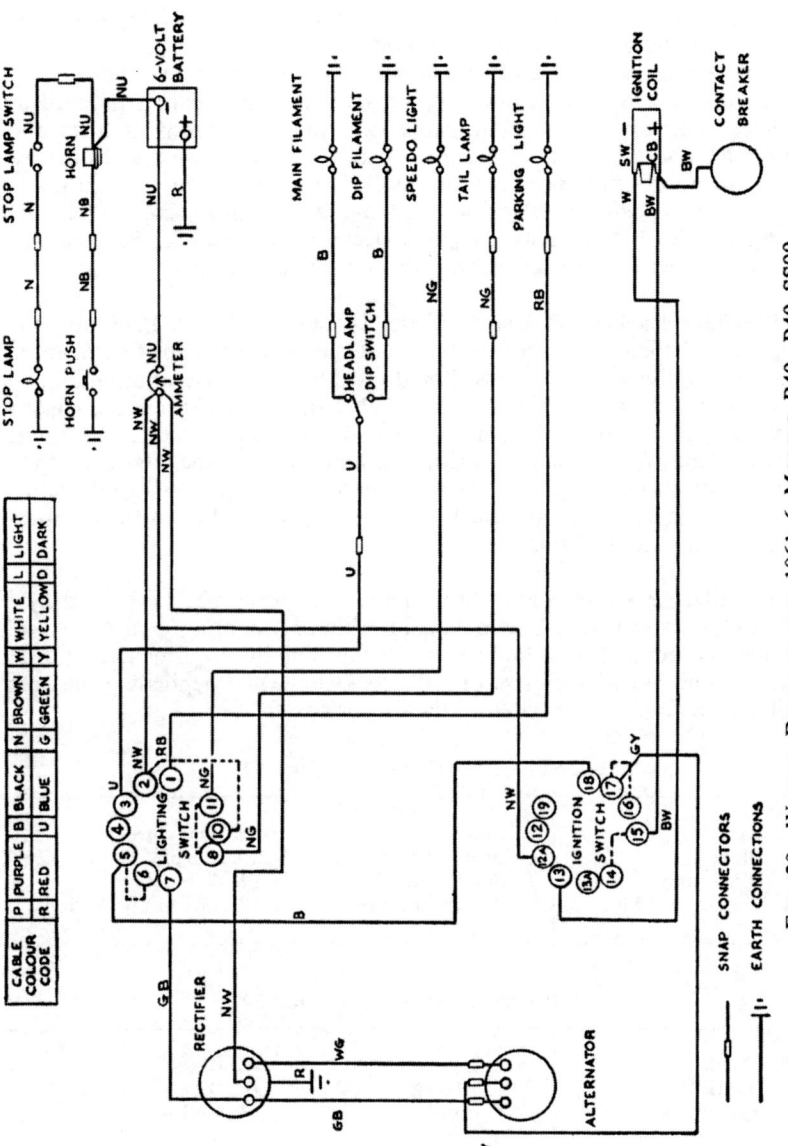

FIG. 20. WIRING DIAGRAM FOR 1961–6 MODELS B40, B40 SS90

All cables to the headlamp are taken directly into the switch, which can be easily withdrawn from the lamp body. The various lighting cables are identified by means of coloured sleeves, or by colours on the harness. When making a connexion, proceed as follows: bare about $\frac{3}{8}$ in. of the cable, twist the wire strands together, and turn back about $\frac{1}{8}$ in., so as to form a small ball. Remove the grub-screw from the appropriate terminal and insert the wire so that the ball fits in the terminal post. Now replace and tighten the grub-screw; this will compress the ball to make a good electrical connexion. See that the rubber sleeves are pulled well over the various connectors.

"Factory Exchange" Units. If the harness leads are kept properly clipped or taped to prevent chafing, and the leads are kept free from oil and grease, the wiring harness should last for years without attention. It is desirable, however, about every 15,000 miles (or during a complete overhaul) to remove a dynamo or "Magdyno" and submit it to a Lucas service depot for overhaul, lubrication, and an endurance test for condition. If its general condition has deteriorated, you can exchange the faulty unit for a factory-reconditioned unit. The same applies to the compensated-voltage-control unit.

The Electric Horn. Failure to function properly may be caused by a short-circuit in the wiring, a loose connexion or mounting, or a discharged battery. If none of these faults exists, try turning the adjuster screw (at the back of the horn) clockwise or anti-clockwise while depressing the horn button which is incorporated in the dipper switch.

SLEEVE COLOURS, Fig. 19

1. Red	5. Blue	9. Dark green
2. Black	6. Brown and white	10. Purple
3. Black and brown	7. Black and white	11. White
4. Brown and blue	8. Brown and green	12. Green and yellow

SLEEVE COLOURS, Fig. 20

B. Black	L. Light	R. Red
D. Dark	N. Brown	U. Blue
G. Green	P. Purple	Y. Yellow

Running Minus Battery. With Lucas a.c. lighting/ignition, first remove battery, earth its negative lead and disconnect stop-light.

CHAPTER IV

B.S.A. LUBRICATION

A dry sump lubrication system is provided on all 1955–66 350 c.c., 500 c.c. overhead-valve single-cylinder engines. Instructions contained in this chapter and on page 122 are fully comprehensive.

Five Points to Remember. Whatever B.S.A. model you have, there are five essential points to observe. They are—
1. A new engine must be run-in with great care.
2. Sufficient oil must be kept in circulation.
3. The oil must be of good quality.
4. The oil must be kept clean.
5. Oil dilution must not occur.

Running-in. General advice on running-in the engine during the first 1,000–1,500 miles is given on page 7, and the author would again emphasize the importance of these instructions. With regard to lubrication during the running-in period, the makers recommend the use of some upper-cylinder lubricant (*see* page 8), and it is important to keep the level of oil in the tank high and to change the oil regularly (*see* page 40).

Inspect Oil Level Every 250 Miles. The oil level in the tank of all 1955 and later models should be inspected regularly and the oil replenished if necessary. The tank holds 4–5½ pints. The level of oil in a tank should *never be allowed to fall below the oil level mark on the outside of the tank.* When replenishing, do not fill the tank more than about one inch below the top of the tank, otherwise oil will seep from the filler cap. It would also not be possible to observe properly the oil returning from the engine into the tank.

Suitable Engine Oils. To obtain maximum performance from your B.S.A. engine, with the minimum amount of wear, the manufacturers recommend the use of one of the following high-grade engine oils (not tabulated in any special order)—
1. Castrol XXL (XL during winter).
2. Mobiloil BB (A during winter).
3. Shell X 100–40 (X 100–30 during winter).
4. B.P. Energol SAE 40 (SAE 30 during winter).
5. Esso Motor Oil 40/50 (20W/30 during winter).
6. Regent Havoline SAE 40 (SAE 30 during winter).

DRY SUMP LUBRICATION

Models B31–B34, M33. With slight variations due to differences in tank filters, the same lubrication system is used for all the single-cylinder models. As may be seen in Fig. 22, the lubricating oil is circulated by a double gear pump located in the bottom of the crankcase towards the off-side. Except for the supply and return pipes from the oil tank, all oilways are internal. On the B31–B34 and M33 engines, however, there is also an external feed from the return pipe (*see* Fig. 22) to the overhead rockers.

Engine oil flows from the tank, after permeating its filter (excluding "M" engines), to the top pair of gears comprising the supply pump. It is then pumped past a pressure valve (A, Fig. 22) along the hollow timing-side mainshaft to the big-end roller bearing, and also to the oilways feeding the cam spindles (*see* Fig. 22).

Having lubricated the big-end bearing and circulated throughout the engine, in the form of oil mist, the oil drains down through a filter in the base of the crankcase. From there it is scavenged by the lower pair of gears comprising the return pump, is passed through the ball valve C, and is delivered through the return pipe to the tank. On M33, engines the returning oil passes through a star-shaped filter element in the oil tank. On all other engines the cylindrical gauze filter is on the supply side.

On M33, B31–B34 O.H.V. engines, some of the returning oil is by-passed up the oil feed pipe to the enclosed rockers and valves, the feed pipe being connected by three unions. Surplus oil is returned to the crankcase on 1955–7 engines through the rocker-box oil return pipe which is connected by a union to the base of the inlet valve spring housing. On 1958–60 engines surplus oil flows back through the vertical push-rod cover.

Models B40, B40 SS90. The dry sump lubrication system is operated by a double gear type pump positioned in the base of the crankcase on the off side. Fig. 23 illustrates the system. Engine oil is fed from the oil tank (capacity four pints) to the supply pump which is the top set of gears. The supply pump then forces the oil past the non-return valve (*A*) through the hollow engine mainshaft to the connecting-rod big-end bearing.

After lubricating various parts of the engine the oil flows down through a gauze filter to the base of the crankcase. The return pump which is the lower set of gears then draws the oil past the non-return valve (*C*) and forces it up the return pipe to the oil tank. The overhead valve rockers, push-rod ends, etc, are pressure fed from a by-pass pipe connected to the oil return pipe inside the tank.

Note that the valve (*A*) stops oil being transferred from the oil tank to the crankcase when the engine is stopped. The valve (*A*) and the sludge trap (*F*) need no maintenance or attention until a general overhaul is undertaken. Constant pressure in the lubrication system is maintained by the oil-pressure release valve (*D*), surplus oil being discharged into the crankcase. This valve is referred to on page 122.

Checking the Oil Circulation. To check the oil circulation on all O.H.V. engines, remove the filler cap from the oil tank with the engine ticking over. Then note whether oil issues steadily from the orifice of the oil

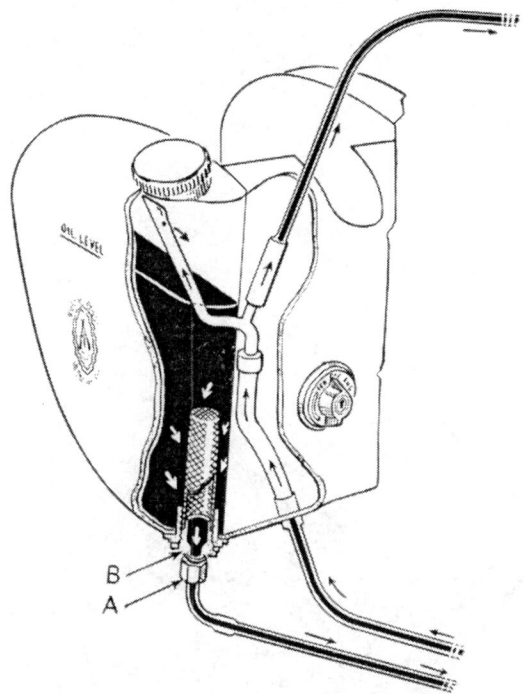

FIG. 21. OIL TANK, FILTER AND ASSOCIATED PIPES ON THE 1961–6 B.S.A. MODELS B40, B40 SS90

A. Supply pipe union nut   *B*. Hexagon plug carrying filter

return pipe. If it does not do so, investigate the reason immediately. Begin by checking the level of oil in the tank (*see* page 35).

Failure of the oil to return to the tank (Models B40, B40 SS90) may be due to the ball valve shown at (*C*) in Fig. 23 sticking in its seating. The remedy is to remove the cover plate (*B*) from the under side of the oil pump, insert a piece of wire into the valve orifice and lift the ball off its seating to free it.

Rectifying Lubrication Trouble (B31–B34, M33). Leakage of oil at the filler cap sometimes occurs. This is generally due to excessive pressure

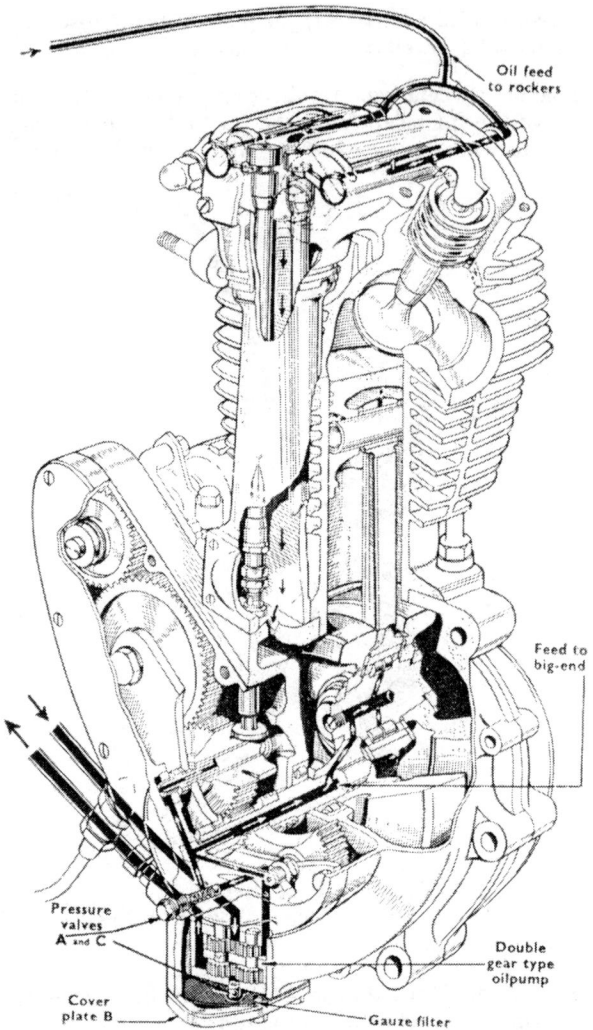

FIG. 22. OIL CIRCULATION (MODELS B31, B32, B33, B34 AND M33)

inside the oil tank. Make sure that the short horizontal pipe on the oil-breather tower (*see* Fig. 24) below the dual seat is unobstructed.

Gradual draining of the oil in the tank to the crankcase is another trouble which is occasionally met. It takes place with the engine not running and is caused through poor seating of the ball valve shown at *A* in Fig. 22. To rectify the trouble, remove the plug over the valve, and detach both the ball and its spring. Clean the ball and its seating, replace the ball, deliver a sharp tap (with a hammer and copper drift) fit the spring, plug, and washer, and then test for oil leakage.

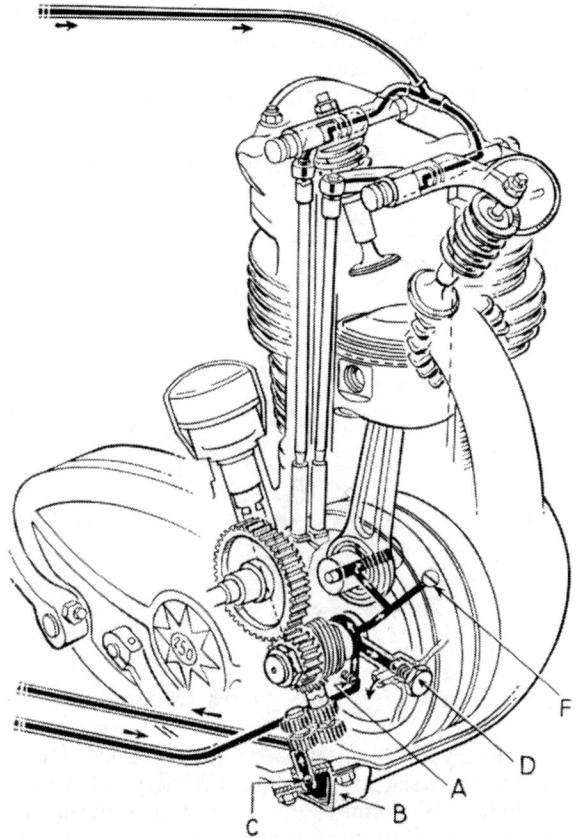

FIG. 23. OIL CIRCULATION (MODELS B40, B40 SS90)

Yet another lubrication trouble is failure of the oil to return to the oil tank due to sticking of the ball valve shown in *C* in Fig. 22. To restore the oil return, remove the cover plate (*B*) from beneath the oil pump, insert some wire into the valve orifice, and free the valve by lifting the ball off its seating.

Oil Loss from Timing Case Breather (B31–34, M33). Check pressure valves *A* and *C* (*see* Fig. 22). If leakage *persists* past valve *A*, lightly grind-in a standard size ball on the seating, using a ball soldered to the end of a 3 in. nail or thin rod. Use only a trace of grinding paste and be sure *all* is afterwards removed. See that the breather diaphragm (a tiny fibre disc) is free and that its polished surface is *uppermost*. Test the breather with the mouth, and adjust the thickness of the washer so that the hole near the top of the pipe faces towards the cover and slightly to the rear. Bad oil loss (experienced by the author) may be caused by oil flooding into the timing case because of worn or perished rubber oil-seals for the camwheel spindles. Renew these (and the spindle bushes also) if necessary.

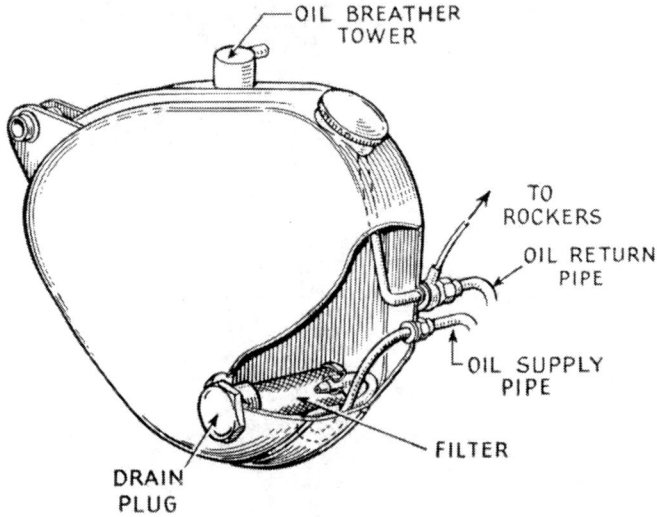

FIG. 24. THE OIL TANK AND FILTER (MODELS B31–B34)

Change the Oil Every 2,000 Miles. About every 2,000 miles, preferably with the engine warm after running, drain off the whole of the oil in the tank. On Models B31–B34 remove the large chromium-plated drain plug to which the horizontal filter is attached (*see* Fig. 24). On Model M33 remove the drain plug shown in Fig. 25. On B40, B40 SS90 disconnect oil pipe union nut shown at *A* in Fig. 21. Then wash the tank out with suitable flushing oil or thin machine oil. Do not employ petrol or paraffin for the purpose. Remove the filter in the oil tank for thorough cleaning; also clean the sump filter. Having cleaned the tank and both filters, replenish the oil tank with the correct grade and brand of engine oil (*see* page 35). On new machines the oil tank should be drained after the first 250 miles and again at 500 miles. Thereafter draining every 2,000 miles is sufficient.

Before draining the oil tank place a fairly large funnel beneath the drain plug and allow the oil to drain off into a receptacle large enough to hold about half a gallon. When replacing a drain plug, be sure to replace the fibre washer.

Cleaning the Tank and Sump Filters. Both filters should be thoroughly washed in petrol or paraffin and dried properly before replacement. No attempt should be made to remove the oil pump itself, unless this is essential for some particular reason. When cleaning the oil tank filter, place the filter in a receptacle of sufficient size to enable it to be completely submerged and never use a rag on it, in case fluff gets caught in the mesh.

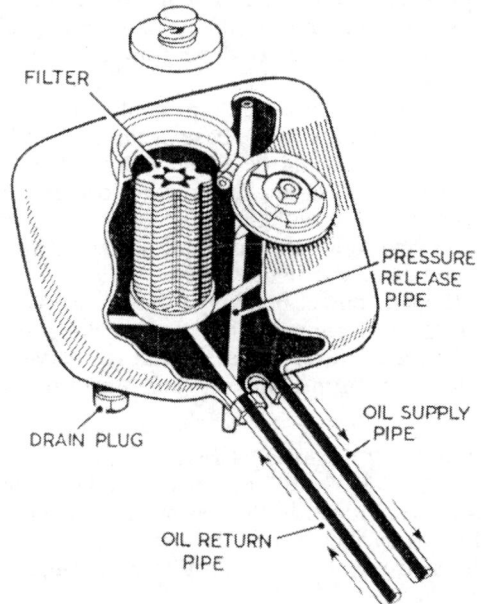

FILTER

PRESSURE RELEASE PIPE

DRAIN PLUG

OIL SUPPLY PIPE

OIL RETURN PIPE

FIG. 25. THE OIL TANK AND FILTER ON MODEL M33

To remove the filter from the oil tank on Model M33, release the tank filler-cap and the spring-loaded cap is thereby exposed. The star-shaped filter (Fig. 25) can then be lifted out for cleaning.

On Models B31–B34 the tank filter is attached to the drain plug shown in Fig. 24, and separate removal is not entailed. On Models B40, B40 SS90 after releasing the oil pipe union nut shown at A in Fig. 21, unscrew the hexagon plug B which carries the filter.

To remove the sump filter (Models B31–B34, M33) remove the nuts securing the cover plate beneath the oil pump and withdraw the flat gauze filter for cleaning (every 2,000 miles). Do not disturb the pump.

When replacing the flat gauze, and cover plate, see that the sump and plate faces are quite clean and fit new paper washers above and below the gauze. Tighten the cover-plate securing nuts evenly and firmly to ensure an oil-tight joint. Tighten again after running. *Avoid excessive leverage*, or the studs will shear. On Models B40, B40 SS90 remove the four self-locking nuts securing the filter/sump unit (integral).

THE "MAGDYNO," DYNAMO, ETC. (1955-7)

"Magdyno" Lubrication. Every Lucas "Magdyno" during assembly has the bearings and gear-wheels packed with grease, and for this reason no lubricators are provided on the instrument. After many thousands of miles' running, when a general overhaul is required, the "Magdyno" should be returned to a Lucas service depot for dismantling, cleaning, and repacking with grease.

The ignition portion has a face-cam type contact-breaker (Fig. 34) and the cam is lubricated by a wick in the base of the contact-breaker. A few drops of thin machine oil should be added every 3,000-4,000 miles. By removing the spring arm carrying the moving contact the small wick-screw can be unscrewed and withdrawn. At the same time remove the contact-breaker securing screw and contact-breaker; withdraw the tappet operating the spring arm, and lightly smear it with a little *thin* machine oil. Replace the tappet, contact-breaker, and also the wick-screw. When replacing the spring arm, see that the small backing spring is located correctly on the *outside* of the spring arm, with the curved portion facing *outwards*. Replace the spring washer and securing screw; tighten firmly.

Oil Leakage from the "Magdyno" Drive. To cure oil leakage from the "Magdyno" drive on 1955-7 "B" and "M" models, slacken the strap and pull the instrument towards the nearside. This ensures the maintenance of a perfect oil seal between the rubber washer and the "Magdyno" pinion. Hold the instrument in this position and re-tighten the securing strap bolt firmly.

Contact-breaker Unit (Models B40, B40 SS90). About every 5,000 miles smear the surface of the cam very lightly with grease. Alternatively some clean engine oil (SAE 30-40) can be used. Referring to Fig. 36 it is important that the weights (*C*) of the centrifugal timing control move freely. Apply a few drops of light oil to the bearings (*E*). Avoid excessive lubrication, otherwise some oil may get on the contacts of the contact-breaker.

Air Filters (Oil-dip Type). Appropriate instructions for dealing with C. & W. oil-dip type air filters fitted to the air-intakes of the carburettors on many 1955-60 models are given on page 16.

THE MOTOR-CYCLE PARTS

Although engine lubrication is obviously of major importance, correct lubrication of motor-cycle parts should not be neglected, otherwise waste of power and undue wear and tear of the transmission and machine will be caused.

Suitable Greases. Grease nipples are provided for motor-cycle parts which need regular greasing, and a Tecalemit grease-gun for grease injection is included in the tool kit. Certain parts require to be lubricated with engine oil (*see* page 35) and oil caps or oil holes with protective spring covers are fitted for this purpose. Always use a high quality grease. Suitable greases, recommended by B.S.A. Motor Cycles, Ltd., are as follows—

1. Mobilgrease MP
2. Shell Retinax A
3. Castrolease LM
4. Esso Multipurpose Grease H
5. B.P. Energrease L2
6. Regent Marfak Multi-purpose 2.

Grease containers designed for quick filling of the grease-gun are available and obviate the messy job of filling the gun by hand. For winter use, Castrolease Medium is suitable as an alternative to Castrolease LM (except for the wheel hubs), and the author finds it can often be more readily injected. After a long run in very rainy weather it is a good plan to apply the grease-gun to all grease nipples, as this will force out any water which may have penetrated into the moving parts.

Lubrication of the Gearbox. On all 1955 and subsequent models B.S.A. gearboxes are specified. These are designed to run on *engine oil only*. Suitable brands of oil are given on page 35. The filler cap or plug (shown in Figs. 68 and 26 respectively) on the off side of the gearbox should be removed and the oil level checked about every 1,500 miles; top-up with sufficient engine oil.

When replenishing a B.S.A. gearbox, first see that the machine is upright and on level ground. For filling it is advisable to use a small funnel. Complete filling is assisted by slowly operating the kick-starter several times.

On 1961–6 Models B40, B40 SS90 the drain plug incorporates a level plug (*see* Fig. 26). To top-up the gearbox remove the filler plug, take out the level plug, and replenish the gearbox with the correct type of engine oil until it begins to trickle out of the level plug hole.

On the 1955–60 "swinging arm" models an improved type of four-speed gearbox is fitted, and this also has a separate level plug (shown at (K) in Fig. 68). To top-up the gearbox remove the oval cover-plate on the off-side of the gearbox; it is secured by two screws. Then pour in suitable engine oil (*see* page 35) until it begins to trickle from the level-plug orifice. Afterwards make sure that the level plug and the oval cover plate are both screwed home firmly.

Draining the Gearbox. On a brand new machine, after the first 500 miles and thereafter about every 5,000 miles place an oil tray beneath the gearbox, remove the drain plug and allow all the oil to drain off.

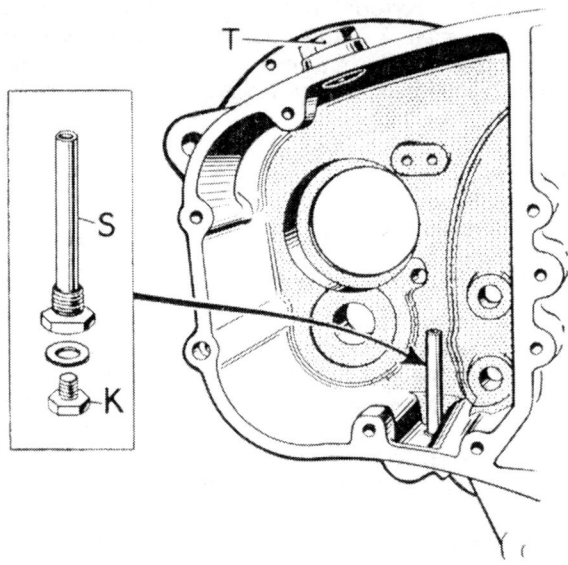

FIG. 26. PROVISION FOR TOPPING-UP AND DRAINING THE
GEARBOX ON 1961–6 MODELS B40, B40 SS90

T. Filler plug   S. Drain plug   K. Level plug

On "swinging arm" models (1955–60) remove the drain plug (shown at (*L*) in Fig. 68), completely drain the gearbox, flush it out with flushing oil, again drain the gearbox, replace the drain plug, and then top-up with suitable engine oil to the level of the hole exposed by removing the level plug (*K*).

On 1961–6, B40, B40 SS90 models it is preferable to drain off the oil while it is warm after a run. Referring to Fig. 26, unscrew the drain plug (*S*), carrying with it the level plug (*K*). Completely drain the gearbox, replace the drain plug, and top-up with suitable engine oil through the hole for the filler plug (*T*) until it begins to flow out through the level plug hole. Do not remove the circular plug adjacent to (*T*).

The Clutch Control. On the 1955–60 "swinging arm" models about every 1,000 miles with the grease gun inject a little grease (*see* page 43) through the nipple shown at (*F*) in Fig. 68. The clutch control-arm needs this occasional attention.

Lubrication of the Primary Chain. Except on "swinging arm" models the primary chain runs in a pressed-steel oil-bath chain case. Every 2,000 miles drain the case and (with the level plug removed) replenish with new oil (*see* page 46) to the level of the plug orifice on the side of the chain case (*see* Fig. 27). Avoid over-filling the case, otherwise the clutch

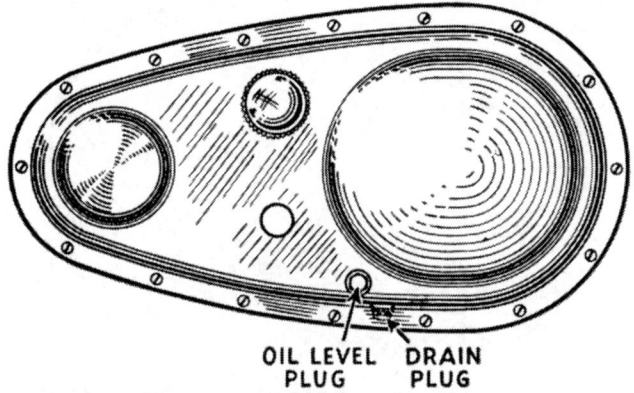

OIL LEVEL   DRAIN
PLUG   PLUG

FIG. 27. THE PRESSED-STEEL OIL-BATH CHAIN CASE (EARLY MODELS)
Its capacity is 2 fluid ounces. An aluminium oil-bath chain case is fitted to
"swinging arm" models.

may slip. When checking the level of oil, make certain that the machine is perfectly upright. Every 300 miles inspect the oil level and top-up.

On 1955–60 "swinging arm" models the primary chain runs in an aluminium oil-bath chain case (*see* Fig. 28). It should be drained and replenished with fresh oil (*see* page 46) every 2,000 miles. Remove the *red-painted* cover fixing screw (*A*) and allow all oil to drain out. Then replace the screw (*A*), remove the cap (*C*), and pour in the oil to the level of the *red-painted* cover fixing screw (*B*) which must be temporarily removed. Note that when the oil-bath is replenished the motor-cycle should be on level ground. with the stand up. It is desirable to inspect the oil level about every 300 miles and top-up if necessary.

On 1961–6 "swinging arm" models (B40, B40 SS90) an aluminium oil-bath chain case is also provided. It is desirable to check the oil level about every 500 miles. Every 5,000 miles drain off the oil and replenish with fresh oil. As may be seen in Fig. 60 a level screw and a drain screw are provided. The level screw (*M*) is painted red, and the drain screw is similarly painted. To top-up the oil-bath chain case place the machine on level ground off its stand and remove the level screw (*M*) and the clutch inspection cover (*H*). Then pour in the oil through the inspection cover hole until oil begins to flow from the level screw hole. Allow sufficient time for surplus oil to drain away. Too much oil causes a tendency for clutch slip. After topping-up replace the level screw and the clutch inspection cover. Be sure to tighten the level screw very securely. The drain and level screws both have fibre washers.

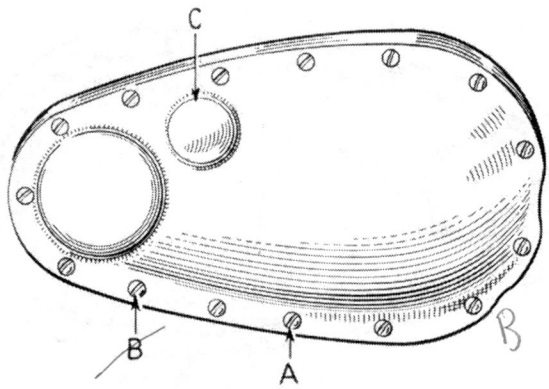

FIG. 28. THE ALUMINIUM OIL-BATH CHAIN CASE (1955–60)

On alternator models use ½ pint of grade S.A.E. 20 engine oil during the summer and winter. Note the outer cover is secured to the chain case (capacity: 8 fluid ounces) by three (larger diameter) short bolts at the front, six long bolts at the rear, and six intermediate size bolts between. *See* also Fig. 60.

Suitable Oils for Primary Chain. Suitable oils for replenishing the oil-bath chain case on all models are: Shell X100–20W, Castrol Castrolite, Mobiloil Arctic, B.P. Energol SAE 20W, Esso Motor Oil 20W/30, and Regent Havoline SAE 20W. Engine oil should not be used.

Lubrication of the Secondary Chain. On 1961–6 Models B40, B40 SS90 the secondary chain is automatically lubricated by a chain oiler at the rear of the primary-chain case. Where no automatic lubrication is provided it is desirable to smear grease with a brush on to the chain about every 500 miles, or whenever the chain seems dry.

Engine oil can be used for the rear chain, and the best method of oiling is to rotate the chain with the wheel and apply an oil-can to the top of the lower chain run. See that the oil is falling upon the rollers, not on the ground, and make a practice of oiling regularly. If the chain is neglected, undue wear of both chain and sprockets will ensue, and the transmission will be harsh. From time to time (say once every 2,000 miles) take off the chain and give it a bath in paraffin. If allowed to soak well, the whole of the dirt will be extracted, and the chain may be hung up to dry before refitting. Cleaning is unnecessary if the chain is fully enclosed.

Before refitting the chain the wisest course is to immerse it in a receptacle containing a mixture of warm graphite and grease, such as Mobilgrease No. 2, which will then permeate all the roller bearings. There is no better treatment for a main driving chain, although plain engine oil or regular greasing will answer satisfactorily. After it has cooled, wipe off the excess lubricant. As the lubricant will be gradually squeezed out under load, the process should therefore be repeated about every 2,000 miles. Clean the sprockets and, on replacing the chain, see that the split end of the spring link faces *opposite* to the direction of the chain travel.

The foregoing instructions are applicable to 1955 and later "swinging arm" models. On 1955–60 "B" models, however, the secondary chain runs in a pressed-steel chain case (where specified). Where total enclosure is provided, remove the front rubber-plug and afterwards apply an oil-can through the inspection hole. When removing the chain for cleaning and greasing (rarely necessary) first remove the rear section of the chain case, and then the upper and lower middle-sections.

The Transmission Shock-Absorber. No lubrication of the engine shaft shock-absorber is needed, as this, being enclosed in the chain case, is adequately lubricated by oil thrown off the primary chain. On alternator models (1958–66) there is no engine-shaft shock-absorber.

The Hub Bearings. About every 1,000 miles apply a grease-gun to the nipples, except on full-width light-alloy hubs. Here it is only necessary to repack the bearings with grease during a complete overhaul. If a sidecar outfit is concerned, do not overlook the hub of the sidecar wheel. Three to four strokes of the gun should be ample. If excessive grease is injected, some of it may get on the brake linings and cause reduced braking power.

The Steering Head Lock. On 1955–66 models having a steering-head lock it is important to note that oil should *not* be inserted into the keyhole. Specially prepared lubricant is introduced during assembly and the subsequent insertion of oil is likely to clog the wards and wash away the special lubricant. It is permissible, however, after a big mileage or under adverse weather conditions to apply a few drops of thin machine-oil to the periphery of the moving drum.

The Steering Head (1955–60). Lubricate the (lower) thrust ball-bearings in the steering head every 1,000 miles by applying the grease-gun to the nipple. Two to three strokes should suffice.

Replenishing the Telescopic Forks (1955 Onwards). All 1955 and later type forks have drain plugs fitted, and it is simpler to replenish

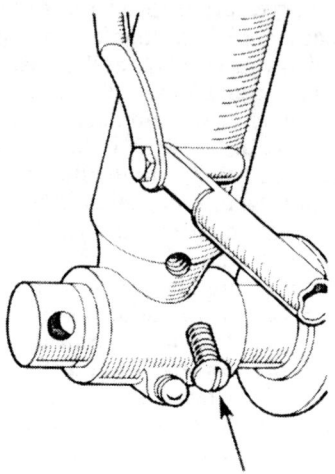

FIG. 29. DRAIN PLUG ON 1955–60 TYPE B.S.A. FORK LEG
The arrow shows the plug removed from the fork leg.

entirely each fork leg rather than to top it up. If excessive up-and-down movement of the forks occurs, replenishment should be effected as described in the following three paragraphs.

First remove the large hexagon-headed cap (and washer) shown at *A* in Fig. 79 from the top of each fork leg. Also remove the small drain plug from the base of the fork leg, drain off all oil, replace the drain plug, and replenish with *five fluid ounces* (142 c.c.)* of new oil. Suitable oils are given below. Although no ill effects will follow replenishing with slightly more than the stipulated amount, it is essential not to exceed the amount by a large extent. If each leg is filled right up it will cease to provide good suspension. A suitable glass measure and small funnel can be obtained from a hardware store. Do *not* replenish with engine oil.

Suitable Oils for Telescopic Front Forks. Use one of the oils mentioned on page 46 for the primary chain.

Draining the Telescopic Front Forks. A tip to remember when draining 1955 and later telescopic-type front forks is that *complete* draining is

* On Models B32, B34 Comp., and 1955–60 "swinging arm" models, the total amount of oil should be 7½ fluid ounces (213 c.c.) of an SAE 20 oil. On 1961–6 Models B40, B40 SS90 replenish each fork leg with ⅓ pint (190 c.c.).

facilitated by standing astride the machine, grasping the handlebars, and working the forks up and down. Drain and replenish every 10,000 miles.

Exposed Cables, Control Levers, and Joints. To prevent corrosion and to ensure smooth action, apply a few drops of oil weekly.

The Speedometer Drive. Every 5,000 miles apply the grease-gun to the speedometer gearbox nipple. Give only two strokes. It is a good plan occasionally to unscrew the knurled ring nut attaching the drive to the

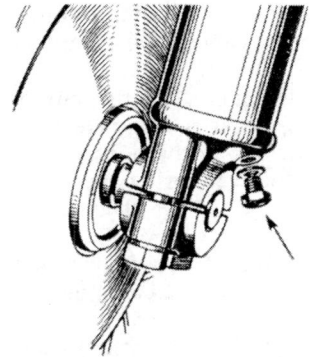

FIG. 30. DRAIN PLUG ON 1961–6 B.S.A. FRONT FORK LEG
This applies to Models B40, B40 SS90.

speedometer, carefully pull the drive clear, and then squirt some oil down between the drive and the outer casing. When reconnecting the drive, see that the connexion goes properly home without force before the ring nut is tightened.

The Spring Frame (Plunger Type). A single nipple is provided for each rear fork leg and about every 500 miles apply the grease-gun. Give several strokes with the gun. It should always be possible to feel a thin film of grease on the upper part of the chromium-plated telescopic member. Wear and rusting will otherwise occur.

The Rear Brake Pedal. Each week apply a few drops of oil to the lubrication hole for the brake-pedal shaft. Apply a little thin oil to the stop-light switch mechanism occasionally.

Lubrication of Brake Cross-over Shaft. The cross-over shaft for the rear brake on 1955–60 "swingers" is well smeared with grease during assembly. After a considerable mileage it is advisable to remove the shaft, wipe it clean, and smear it with fresh grease prior to replacing it.

To remove the cross-over shaft, it is necessary first to disconnect the rear-brake pedal and the cross-over shaft lever. Loosen the pinch-bolts and pull the levers away from the shaft, noting their exact positions to ensure correct re-assembly. *This is most important.* Then pull the cross-over shaft out of the swinging-arm member.

The Brake Cam Spindles. Every 2,000 miles approximately, grease the brake cam spindles. One shot of grease is sufficient.

The Front Brake. Besides oiling the handlebar controls each week (along with the other lever controls), do not omit to oil lightly both ends of the exposed portion of the cable running parallel with the front fork legs.

The Sidecar Chassis. When greasing the hubs of the motor-cycle wheels about every 1,000 miles, or at a complete overhaul (light-alloy hubs), remember to lubricate the hub of the sidecar. Also about every 250 miles apply the grease gun to the rear spring and shackle-link bolts. If special instructions are issued by the sidecar makers, follow these closely.

The Central or Rear Stand. Central spring-up stands are fitted to all models, and should be oiled every 2,000 miles.

The Dipper Switch. Every 5,000 miles lubricate the moving parts of the dipper switch with a little *thin* oil. Be careful, or you may cause a short.

"Swinging Arm" Rear Suspension. The hydraulic dampers require no lubrication or other maintenance. On 1961–6 Models B40, B40 SS90 grease the "swinging arm" pivot at intervals of 500 miles. A suitable grease is Mobilgrease Special. Apply grease until it begins to exude from the "swinging arm" bushes. Afterwards wipe away all grease from external surfaces.

CHAPTER V

GENERAL MAINTENANCE

IN this chapter the author has included *all* essential information about the maintenance, dismantling, and assembling of 1955 and later models. Detailed reference to carburation, lubrication, and the lighting system has, however, been omitted, since these subjects have already been fully discussed. To assist the reader in finding what he needs quickly, the chapter has been sub-divided into a number of main sections.

Spares and Repairs. When you have to forward or deliver parts to the makers (B.S.A. Motor Cycles, Ltd., Service Dept., Armoury Road, Birmingham, 11) or to an appointed B.S.A. dealer, remember to attach to each part a label bearing clearly your *full name and address*. Correspondence concerning technical advice and repairs should always be written on separate sheets to ensure prompt attention. To assist identification, also always quote the year and model of machine, and the engine or frame number according to which is applicable.

A useful spares list is obtainable from B.S.A. Motor Cycles, Ltd., or from an appointed spares stockist. Throughout the U.K. there are over 200 of these stockists who maintain a comprehensive stock of B.S.A. spares. Among those in the London area may be mentioned: Whitbys of Acton, Ltd.; Kays of Ealing, Ltd.; Godfreys, Ltd.; Eleanor Motors; F. Parks & Son, Ltd.; Writers, Ltd., Glanfield Lawrence, Ltd.; Owen Bros.; E. S. Longstaff, Ltd.; Cleare & Co., Ltd.; Harry Nash Motors, Ltd.; Slocombes, Ltd.; West End Motors, Ltd.; Elite Motors, and also the firms below marked with an asterisk.

Some Large Accessory Firms. Eight large accessory firms (some of which have branches throughout the U.K.) handling motor-cycle accessories, equipment, proprietary spares, tools, clothing, etc., are: Marble Arch Motor Supplies, Ltd.; The Halford Cycle Co., Ltd.; James Grose, Ltd.*; Turner's Stores*; George Grose, Ltd.*; Claude Rye, Ltd.*; Pride & Clarke, Ltd.; and Whitbys of Acton, Ltd.*

Items Required for Maintenance. Some items besides the standard tool kit you *must* have handy in the lock-up or garage. These include: a can of paraffin for cleaning purposes; a stiff brush for scouring dirt off the crankcase and underneath the motor-cycle; a tin of suitable engine oil for the engine and gearbox (*see* page 35); a small funnel for topping-up the gearbox; a canister of grease (*see* page 43); a receptacle for oil when draining the oil tank; some dishes or jars for washing parts in; some non-fluffy rags; valve-grinding paste such as Richford's (coarse and fine); some fine emery cloth; a set of engine gaskets. You should also have: a pair of new gudgeon-pin circlips; a good valve-spring compressor (*see* page 79) for removing valves. A gudgeon-pin extractor (*see* page 81) is useful, and it is desirable to obtain a wire brush.

Other very desirable items which the author strongly recommends be bought are shown in Fig. 31. Items 1, 4, 5, 6, 8, 10 are really essential, and the remainder form very useful additions to the standard B.S.A. tool kit. The whole of these items do not cost very much, and the author has found them to be worth-while additions. You are also likely to need a "Magdyno" pinion extractor for 1955–57 models (*see* page 85) and an extractor for the clutch centre (*see* page 98).

For the maintenance of the motor-cycle parts you should obtain: a box of spare chain links and a chain rivet extractor; a syringe for topping-up the battery; a hydrometer for checking the specific gravity of the battery electrolyte (*see* page 26); a chamois leather; a sponge and pail (if a hose is not available); some soft dusters (preferably of the Selvyt type); a tin of good wax or other polish for the enamelled parts; and a tin of hand cleanser.

Tools for Repair Work. If you decide to undertake as much repair work as possible besides routine maintenance, stripping-down, and assembly, it is desirable to rig up a suitable bench, complete with vice, and to purchase some extra tools.

To begin, it is a good plan to buy a medium-weight hammer, a hand-drill and an assortment of twist-drills, a hacksaw, some large and small (smooth and rough) files, and a good soldering outfit for the repair of control cables. Repair work is beyond the scope of this handbook, and you need fair technical knowledge and skill in handling tools.

If rebushing of the engine and other components is undertaken, this will necessitate the use of suitable extractors, punches, etc. A number of B.S.A. special service tools may also be obtained if required.

Keep Your B.S.A. Clean. Keep your mount nice and clean. Doubtless it cost quite a sum, and it is well worth careful looking after. With regular and proper cleaning it will function better, will last longer. maintain its good looks, and retain a good market value. A dirty motor-cycle is an eyesore. and remember that dirt hides defects, encourages rusting, and is a menace when stripping down. Never leave your B.S.A. soaking wet overnight. If you have no time for cleaning in wet weather, grease the machine all over *before* use.

Cleaning the Engine and Gearbox. See that the cylinder barrel and cylinder-head fins are kept clean. If the enamel has worn away, paint the barrel fins with some proprietary cylinder black after thorough cleaning with a stiff brush dipped in paraffin. Note that rusted fins, besides looking shabby, cause an appreciable loss in heat dispersion.

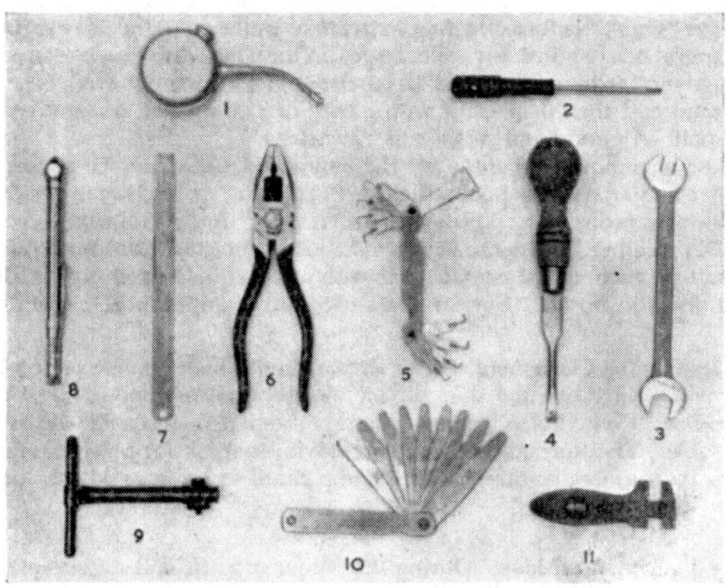

FIG. 31. SOME USEFUL ADDITIONS TO THE STANDARD TOOL KIT

Various items added by the author to his own Model B31 tool kit.
1. Oil can (for engine oil)
2. Small screwdriver
3. Garrington double-ended spanner ($\frac{5}{16}$ in. and $\frac{1}{4}$ in. W.).
Fits acorn nuts at base of push-rod cover tube, rocker-box cover nuts, secondary chain adjusters, sump filter cover-plate nuts (see Fig. 22), and battery strap securing-bolt
4. Medium-size screwdriver
5. Sparking plug re-gapping tool and plug point gauges. Champion and Lodge tools are available (see also Fig. 32)
6. Pliers (with wire cutter)
7. Six-inch steel rule
8. Tyre pressure gauge (6–50 lb per sq in.)*
9. Valve-grinding tool (not required if suction tool (Fig. 48) is provided)
10. A good set of feeler gauges
11. Small adjustable spanner

* The tyre pressure gauge illustrated is a Dunlop pencil type No. 6. Other suitable gauges are the Schrader No. 7750, the Holdtite, and the Romac.

Scour off all filth from the lower part of the engine and gearbox with stiff brushes and paraffin. Clean all aluminium alloy and bright surfaces first with a rag damped in paraffin, assisted by brushes where necessary, and then with a dry rag.

Cleaning the Enamel. Never attempt to remove mud from the enamelled parts when dry and caked, as this is likely to damage the surfaces. Soak the mud off with a hose if available. In the case of a very dirty machine it may be advisable to paint the surfaces over with a cleaning compound such as "Gunk" before directing a stream of water on to the dirty surfaces. Be careful not to allow any water to get on the wheel hub-bearings, and the "Magdyno" (where fitted) and carburettor. If a hose is not available, soak the mud and then disperse it with plenty of clean water, using a sponge and pail. A good hand cleanser is "Swarfega."

Having removed all dirt, dry the enamelled surfaces with a chamois leather and afterwards polish them with soft dusters and some good wax polish or a proprietary polish such as "Karpol" or "Autobrite."

"Dry weather" riders can keep a machine in almost showroom condition merely by rubbing the enamel over with a paraffin-damped rag, followed by a dry, soft duster. For tar spots use cloth damped with turpentine.

Cleaning the Chromium. Never employ liquid metal polish or paste, as this will wear down the thin surface. A good chromium-cleaning compound such as "Belco" can be used, though too frequent use is not desirable. The normal method of removing tarnish (salt deposits) is to clean the surfaces regularly with a damp chamois leather and then polish them with soft dusters.

To Reduce Tarnishing. During the winter months it is a good plan to wipe over occasionally all surfaces with a soft cloth soaked in a proprietary anti-tarnish preparation. An example is "Tekall," obtainable in ½-pint and 1-pint tins.

Petrol-tank Enamel. Occasionally a B.S.A. owner may have the misfortune to scratch or damage a small portion of the tank enamel. Matching up colours is notoriously difficult, and it is worth noting that B.S.A. Motor Cycles, Ltd. supply their spares stockists with small tins of quick-drying cellulose paint of the *exact* colour required (also "Tipon pencils" for general touching-up).

Regularly Check Nuts for Tightness. This is particularly important during running-in (*see* page 7), as some "bedding down" of parts occurs. Regularly apply spanners to the various external nuts to ensure tightness, paying special attention to the engine bolts and nuts, the engine mounting nuts, and the pipe unions. After running-in check them about every 2,000 miles, but after decarbonizing and running for about 250 miles, check the cylinder-head bolts or nuts for tightness, tightening diagonally. Do not use spanners of greater length than the standard ones when tightening nuts, especially those on the crankcase studs.

Carburettor Maintenance and Tuning. For detailed instructions, *see* Chapter II.

B.S.A. Lubrication. Detailed instructions for the lubrication of 1955 and later models are given in Chapter IV.

CARE OF THE IGNITION SYSTEM

All 1955–57 B.S.A. O.H.V. models have Lucas "Magdyno" lighting and ignition equipment provided. For all practical purposes the magneto and dynamo portion (used for lighting only) of the "Magdyno" are separate units. They are united only by a strap and can be separated (*see* page 20).

All 1958–66 O.H.V. models have coil instead of magneto ignition, with a Lucas alternator and rectifier (*see* page 21) supplying current to a battery (below the dual seat) which delivers current for both lighting and ignition. A separate contact-breaker is provided on the off side of the machine instead of on the near side where it was formerly located on the magneto. The rectifier and coil are fitted above the tool compartment.

The maintenance of the E3L dynamo, the alternator, the rectifier, and the battery, has already been dealt with in Chapter III. It remains to cover those components concerned solely with ignition.

Suitable Sparking Plugs. To obtain easy starting and maximum performance throughout the throttle range, it is essential always to run on a suitable sparking plug. Four reliable makes of sparking plugs are the Champion, the Lodge, the K.L.G. and the N.G.K. All 1955 and subsequent engines require 14 mm size plugs, and suitable types are—

1955–60 Models B31–B34, M33. Suitable sparking plugs are the Champion L7, the Lodge H14, and the K.L.G. F70. These 14 mm. sparking plugs have a $\frac{1}{2}$ in. reach

1961–6 Models B40, B40 SS90. B.S.A. Motor Cycles Ltd. recommend the use of the Champion N5 and N4 respectively. These 14 mm. sparking plugs both have a reach of $\frac{3}{4}$ in. and their Lodge and K.L.G. equivalents are the HLN and FE80 respectively.

NGK Sparking Plugs. These excellent non-detachable type plugs can be obtained from most accessory firms and large garages in the U.K. Successfully used by the winners of the 1967 250, 350 and 500 c.c. motorcycle T.T. races in the Isle of Man, they differ basically from their English equivalents in that their centre electrodes are made of copper. The 14 mm. NGK plug recommended for the 1955–60 Models B31–B34 and Model B33 is the B-7H or B-7HC, with a $\frac{1}{2}$ in. reach; that recommended for the

1961–6 Models B40 and B40 SS90 is the B–7E or B–7EC, with a ¾ in. reach.

Keep the Plug Gap Correct. This is extremely important. It is advisable to check the plug gap about every 1,000 miles and to adjust the gap if burning of the points has caused the gap to exceed 0·020 in. B.S.A. Motor Cycles Ltd. recommend a gap of 0·018–0·020 in.* For obvious reasons, when re-gapping it is best to set the gap at the *bottom* limit. Check the gap with a wire or feeler gauge such as those shown at (5) and (10) respectively in Fig. 31. The gauge should just enter without friction.

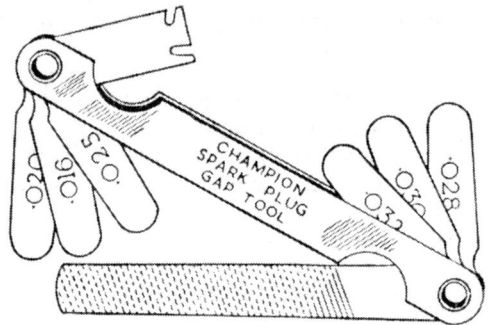

FIG. 32. A HANDY CHAMPION TOOL FOR RE-GAPPING PLUGS
A fine file is provided for brightening-up plug points.

When adjusting the plug gap, never attempt to bend or tap the centre electrode. Use a pair of snipe-nose pliers, or a Champion or Lodge re-gapping tool (Fig. 32), to bend the outside (earth) electrode. Tapping the earth electrode is not a good method. When the plug has to be thoroughly cleaned, do this as described opposite, and *then* re-gap.

Cleaning the Sparking Plug. If carburation is correct and excessive oil is not entering the combustion chamber, it should not be necessary to inspect and clean the sparking plug thoroughly more often than about once every 2,000 miles. When running-in a new or rebored engine, however, it is advisable to remove and check the plug for cleanliness at intervals of about 500 miles.

Quick cleaning of a plug can be done by brushing the points and lightly rubbing their firing sides with some smooth glass-paper. Alternatively the plug can be cleaned with a proprietary gadget, comprising a metal reservoir, containing steel wires and petrol, into which the plug is screwed and then shaken.

* The recommended gaps for Models B40, B40 SS90 is 0·020 in.–0·025 in.

Cleaning Lodge and K.L.G. Plugs. Fig. 33 shows a typical detachable type (K.L.G.) sparking plug dismantled for thorough cleaning. To dismantle a detachable-type sparking plug, grip the hexagon *E* of the plug body in a vice or with a box spanner. If you use a vice, be most careful not to exert any pressure on the hexagon faces. Then with a suitable spanner (preferably a box or ring spanner), unscrew the small hexagon *B*, being careful not to distort the integral metal body. The centre electrode *F* with its insulation (comprising the insulated electrode assembly *A*) can now be detached from the gland nut. Take care not to lose the internal sealing-washer *H*.

To clean the "Sintox" or "Corundite" insulation, used on Lodge and K.L.G. plugs respectively, wipe it clean with a cloth soaked in petrol or paraffin. If the insulation is coated with hard carbon deposits, remove these with some fine glass-paper, but make no attempt to scrape off the deposits. The internal sealing-washer *H* and the surfaces on the insulator and in the metal body on which this washer rests are very important, as they prevent gas leakage through the plug. Therefore wipe them only with a rag soaked in petrol or paraffin. Any damage caused while dismantling will render the plug unserviceable.

To clean the metal parts (plug body and gland nut), wipe them clean with petrol, or, if necessary, scrape off the deposits with a small knife, or use a wire brush. Afterwards rinse the parts in petrol. The gland nut seldom gets very fouled, but the inside of the plug body may be very dirty, and the same may apply to the external threads of the plug. Clean and polish the points of the centre and outside (earth) electrodes *F* and *G* (Fig. 33) with some fine glass-paper.

See that there is no dirt or grit lodged between the body of the plug and the insulation, and particularly on the internal sealing-washer and the contacting faces. Smear a little thin oil on the internal washer and make sure that it seats properly. When assembling the sparking plug, see that the centre electrode and insulation are positioned centrally in the body bore. If not, remove, re-position by rotating the centre a quarter of a turn, and reassemble. Do not attempt to force or bend them into position.

Tighten the gland nut into the plug body only with a single-handed normal pressure applied to the tommy-bar of the box spanner or ring spanner. It is not advisable to use an open type spanner; this may exert excessive pressure, which will result in distortion of the gland nut and possible damage to the insulation. Finally, it should be verified that the plug gap is correct.

Non-detachable Plugs. A Champion or an NGK non-detachable plug cannot be dismantled and cleaned like the detachable Lodge and K.L.G. plugs. Quick cleaning is, of course, done in the same manner (*see* page 56). The best method of cleaning a non-detachable plug well is to take it to a nearby garage having an "air-blast" unit. In a matter of a few minutes the plug can be thoroughly cleaned of all deposits, washed, subjected to a high-pressure air line, and subsequently tested for sparking at a pressure exceeding 100 lb per sq in.

Keep the tip and outside of the insulation thoroughly clean. After

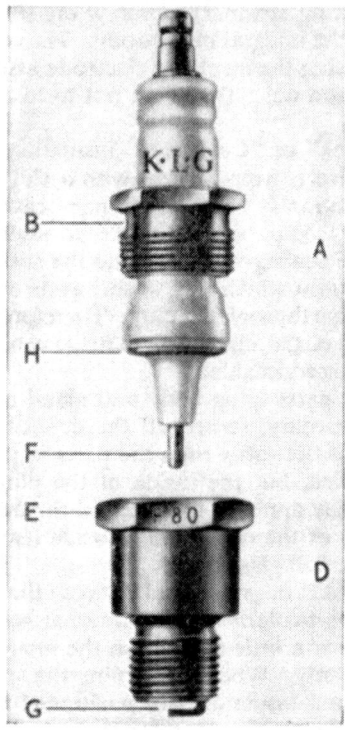

FIG. 33. DETACHABLE TYPE SPARKING PLUG (K.L.G.) DISMANTLED FOR THOROUGH CLEANING

The gland nut *B* and the internal washer *H* are shown still in position on the insulation.

removing all carbon, polish the electrodes with some fine glass-paper. Finally check the plug gap. Detachable Lodge and K.L.G. plugs can, also, be quickly dealt with on an "air-blast" unit.

Replacing the Sparking Plug. Before replacing the plug, renew a *copper* gasket if it is worn or flattened, and clean the plug threads. Screw the plug home by hand as far as possible, and always use the box spanner for final tightening. An adjustable spanner should not be used. *Steel* Champion gaskets do *not* need renewal.

Keep the "Magdyno" Contact-breaker Gap Correct. Little attention to the ignition portion of the Lucas "Magdyno" is needed, other than occasional lubrication (*see* page 42) and attention to the face-cam type contact-breaker, shown in Fig. 34. Any serious internal trouble should be dealt with by a Lucas service depot.

The contacts of the contact-breaker (Fig. 34) should be examined about every 3,000 miles. If the "break," with the contacts fully open is appreciably more, or less, than will just take a 0·012–0·015 in. blade of a feeler gauge, the contacts should be adjusted (*after* cleaning, if necessary). Too

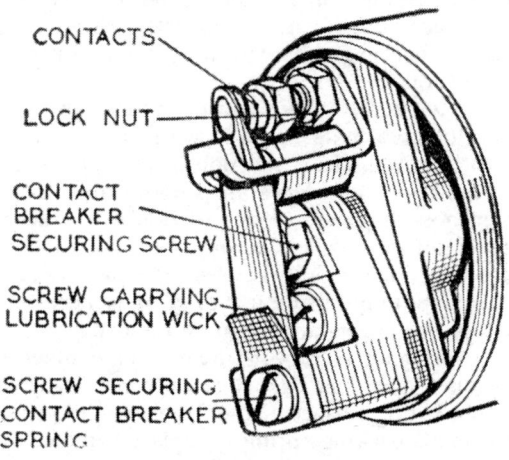

CONTACTS

LOCK NUT

CONTACT BREAKER SECURING SCREW

SCREW CARRYING LUBRICATION WICK

SCREW SECURING CONTACT BREAKER SPRING

FIG. 34. THE FACE-CAM TYPE CONTACT-BREAKER USED ON LUCAS "MAGDYNOS" (1955–7)

great a gap will advance the timing. The magneto spanner gauge or the blade of a proprietary set of feelers can be useful for checking the "break," the procedure for which is as follows—

1. Remove the contact-breaker cover and rotate the engine slowly forwards until the contacts of the contact-breaker are wide open (near T.D.C. on the firing stroke).

2. Insert the blade of the feeler gauge between the contacts.

3. If the feeler gauge *just* slides in without friction, the gap is correct and no adjustment is needed. If the gauge is a slack fit or the contacts have to be sprung to enable it to enter, adjust the gap as follows.

4. With the magneto spanner loosen the lock-nut which secures the stationary-contact screw (*see* Fig. 34) and then adjust this screw by means of its hexagon head until the correct gap is obtained between the fixed (outer) and adjustable (inner) contacts.

5. Re-tighten the contact screw lock-nut and again check the gap. If correct, replace the contact-breaker cover.

Cleaning the "Magdyno" Contacts. At intervals of about 3,000 miles, when checking the contact-breaker gap, scrutinize the contacts closely. If the contacts are allowed to become dirty or oily, rapid burning, pitting, and consequent ignition trouble will ensue.

If inspection reveals that the contacts have a *grey*, *frosted* appearance, with no blackening or pitting, do not interfere with them (assuming that the gap is correct). If the contacts are only slightly discoloured, clean them with a rag moistened with petrol.

On examination after a big mileage the contacts may be found to have irregular and blackened areas due to pitting and burning (especially if the contacts have not been kept clean and correctly adjusted). In this case it is essential to clean them up, otherwise misfiring and rapid deterioration of the contacts will follow.

To clean the contacts, use a *fine* carborundum slip or a piece of *fine* emery cloth (do not use a nail file), and with the contact-breaker spring arm (*see* Fig. 34) removed, clean and polish the contacts until all pitting disappears and the contact surfaces are smooth all over. Be careful to keep the contact faces "square" as well as uniform. *This is most important.** If pitting is not serious, it is perhaps best not to remove the spring arm, but to insert the emery cloth between the two contacts, while both are in position. If pitting is serious, or if it is necessary to examine contacts effectively, the spring arm must be removed.

To remove the spring arm (carrying the moving contact) on a face-cam type contact-breaker (*see* Fig. 34), it is only necessary to remove the securing screw and spring washer. When replacing the spring arm, make certain that the small backing spring is replaced immediately under the securing screw and spring washer, with the curved portion facing *outwards* as shown in Fig. 34. See that the contacts are perfectly aligned before tightening the securing screw firmly.

Where very deep pitting is present, it may be necessary to remove the complete contact-breaker after detaching the spring arm. To do this, unlock the tab-washer and remove the contact-breaker securing screw, when the complete contact-breaker can be withdrawn, and dealt with on a bench or table if desired. When replacing the contact-breaker, see that a new tab-washer is fitted and locked over the securing screw. It is not advisable to remove much metal from the contacts, and if a reasonable amount of facing-up fails to restore the surfaces to normal, fit a new pair of contacts (including, of course, a new spring arm). After dealing with the contacts as described, wipe away any metal dust with a petrol-dampened cloth and check the gap.

The "Magdyno" Slip-ring. Moisture, oil, or dirt accumulating on the slip-ring is liable to cause difficult starting and misfiring. About every

---

* Note that the later type Lucas contacts have slightly convex (not flat) faces, must which be cleaned with fine emery cloth only.

2,000 miles (when cleaning both filters) remove the h.t. pick-up from the "Magdyno" and thoroughly clean the flanges and track of the slip-ring. Do this by holding a soft, dry cloth, wrapped round a pencil, through the pick-up hole, and, with the cloth lightly pressed against the slip-ring, slowly turn the engine. The h.t. pick-up is secured to the body of the "Magdyno" by two small screws. The near-side screw is rather inaccessible on some models, and to remove and tighten both screws it is necessary first to remove the oil tank.

The H.T. Pick-up. When cleaning the slip-ring, also clean the surface of the pick-up moulding with a cloth moistened with petrol, and polish

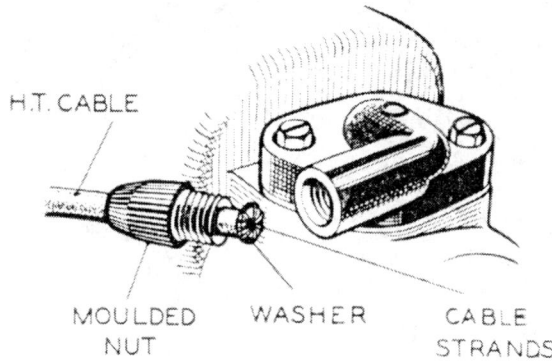

H.T. CABLE

MOULDED   WASHER   CABLE
NUT   STRANDS

FIG. 35. RENEWING H.T. CABLE ON LUCAS "MAGDYNO"

with a fine, dry cloth. Examine the pick-up moulding for cracks, and closely inspect the spring and carbon brush. The brush must move freely in its holder, but be careful not to stretch the spring. Renew the spring at once if it has weakened, and always renew a badly worn brush. When replacing the h.t. pick-up moulding, do not forget to replace the small gasket. Examine the earth brush (held by a cheese-head screw).

Renewing the H.T. Cable. When renewing a cracked or perished h.t. cable, utilize 7 mm plastic-covered ignition cable. Bare the end of the cable (*see* Fig. 35) for about $\frac{1}{4}$ in. and thread the cable through the moulded terminal nut. Pass the wire through the bronze washer and then bend back the cable strands as illustrated. Finally screw the moulded terminal-nut into the pick-up connexion.

The Contact-breaker Gap (1958–60 Models B31–B34, M33). The contact-breaker assembly on the 1958–60 350 c.c. and 500 c.c. coil-ignition models is shown in Fig. 55. Always maintain the gap between the contacts at 0·012–0·015 in. An adjustment is normally necessary only at long intervals (about every 3,000 miles), but during the running-in period the gap should be checked after the first few hundred miles.

Referring to Fig. 55, to make a contact-breaker adjustment, rotate the engine until the contacts are wide open and insert the appropriate blades of a set of feeler gauges between the contacts. Should the gap be found incorrect, loosen the screw E and move the plate F gently with a screw-driver until the gap is 0·012–0·015 in. Afterwards firmly tighten screw E and again check the contact-breaker gap.

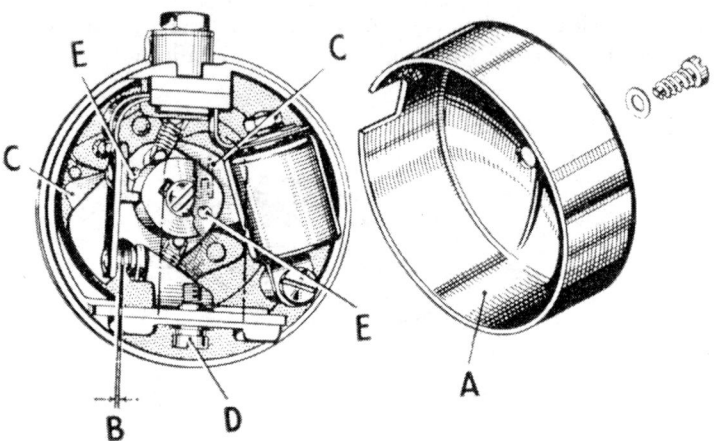

FIG. 36. LUCAS CONTACT-BREAKER ON 1961–4 MODELS B40,
B40 SS90

The C.B./ignition-advance unit is behind the cylinder. For 1965 C.B. *see* Fig. 84.

Cleaning the Contacts (1958–60 Models B31–B34, M33). Cleaning is necessary only at long intervals, but when checking the contact-breaker gap it is desirable to inspect the contacts to see that they are clean and not blackened or pitted (*see* page 60). Slightly discoloured contacts can be cleaned with a rag moistened with petrol, but thorough cleaning should be effected by withdrawing the moving contact and cleaning both contacts with a fine carborundum slip or some fine emery cloth.

The Contact-breaker Gap (1961–4 Models B40, B40 SS90). The contact-breaker and its automatic ignition-advance mechanism is in a self-contained unit mounted above the crankcase behind the cylinder. Always maintain the gap between the contacts at 0·015 in. Check the gap after completing 500 miles during the running-in period and subsequently about every 2,000 miles. For 1965–6 contact-breaker gap details, *see* page 122.

Referring to Fig. 36, remove the contact-breaker cover A. Take out the sparking plug to facilitate the engine being turned over by hand operation of the kick-starter and slowly turn the engine over until the gap *B* between the contacts is at its maximum. Check the gap with a suitable feeler gauge and adjust as required to 0·015 in. The fixed contact is attached to a plate mounted at right angles to the moving contact. If an adjustment is necessary, slacken screw *D* and move the plate until the feeler gauge shows the gap to be correct. Afterwards securely tighten screw *D*, and again check the gap, *essential* to correct ignition timing.

When checking the contact-breaker gap also inspect the contacts and note if they are blackened or pitted. Clean the contacts with a fine carborundum stone or emery cloth, afterwards wiping the contacts with a cloth moistioned in petrol. Cleaning is usually *needed* every 5,000 miles.

The Battery. On all the coil-ignition models it is important to keep the battery in good condition owing to the dual demands made upon it for lighting and ignition.

Attention to the Coil. The Lucas coil used on coil-ignition models requires no attention whatever other than occasional cleaning of the exterior, especially the space between the terminals. See that the connexions at the terminals are kept tight, and the wiring is in good condition. On 1958–66 models the coil is well protected in the tool box.

Symptoms of a Faulty Condenser. The condenser (which is connected in parallel with the contact-breaker circuit) is primarily designed to prevent arcing between the contacts at the moment of the "break." It rarely develops a defect and the symptoms of condenser trouble are unmistakable—a pronounced tendency for the contacts to become rapidly burnt and pitted, in spite of their being kept clean and correctly adjusted. If such trouble occurs, inspect the condenser immediately.

Automatic Ignition-advance Mechanism. The contact-breaker contacts are opened and closed by a cam on the driving spindle and a centrifugally operated governor controls the relationship of the cam with the spindle. The bob-weights shown at *C* in Fig. 36 must move freely and this can be tested by turning the cam to the advanced position when the bob-weights will be fully extended outwards. If the cam is then released the springs should withdraw the bob-weights to the inner or retarded position. Should the bob-weights be stuck in the retarded position engine performance declines and there is likely to be overheating, accompanied possibly by damage to the exhaust valve. As as been mentioned on page 42, the occasional lubrication of the bob-weight bearings with a few drops of light oil will ensure proper functioning of the ignition-advance mechanism.

VALVE CLEARANCES

It is very important to maintain the correct valve clearances on all B.S.A. engines, and the clearances should be checked about every 2,000 miles when the engine is *quite cold*; after 250 miles in the case of new engines where considerable "bedding down" of the parts occurs; after grinding-in the valves. It should be noted that incorrect valve clearances interfere with both the lift of the valves and also the valve timing.

Excessive clearances result in reduced valve lift and late opening of the valves, which causes undue noise and loss of efficiency, but this is not likely to damage the valves. Insufficient valve clearances, besides resulting in loss of compression, flexibility, and power, may cause distortion and

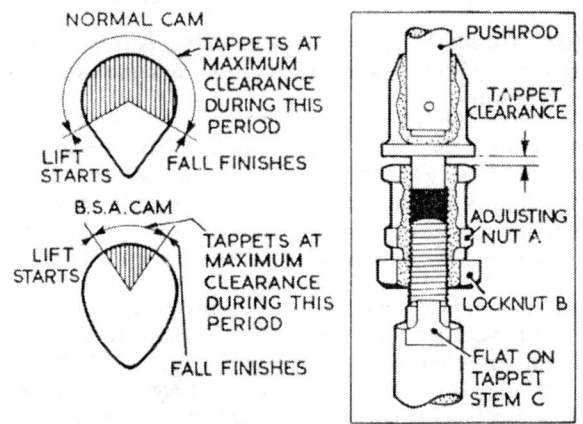

Fig. 37. Tappet Adjustment on Models B31–B34, M33

perhaps burning of the exhaust valve due to gas leakage past it during the power strokes. Experienced riders can usually tell by the sound and "feel" of an engine whether the valve clearances are correct. Before checking the valve clearances it is essential to set the piston at top dead centre and then check that there is sufficient clearance at the exhaust-valve lifter.

Correct Valve Clearances. Valve clearances should always be checked with the engine *cold*. On models B31–B34 and M33 the correct valve clearances (measured with a feeler gauge between the tappet heads and the push-rods) are 0·003 in. for the inlet valve, and 0·003 in. for the exhaust valve.

On Models B40 and B40 SS90 the correct valve clearances (measured with a feeler gauge between the valve stems and the overhead rocker adjusters) are 0·008 in. for the inlet valve, and 0·010 in. for the exhaust valve. The checking and adjustment of the valve clearances are described in the following paragraphs.

Adjustment—Models B31–B34, M20, M21, M33. A similar method of checking and adjusting valve clearances is used for 350 c.c., 500 c.c. O.H.V. engines. On all these engines (which have twin camwheels) the design of the inlet and exhaust cams is such that the foot of each tappet rests on the "neutral" portion of the cam for a comparatively short period (*see* Fig. 37). It is therefore absolutely imperative to make certain that the cams are correctly positioned prior to adjusting the tappets, and to verify that there is sufficient clearance at the exhaust-valve lifter (*see* below). To ensure correct cam positioning, the following procedure must be observed—

Remove the tappet cover and slowly rotate the engine in its normal direction of rotation until the *inlet* valve has just closed (remember by "I see" (I.C.)), the tappet being just free to rotate. Then check the *exhaust* tappet clearance with a suitable feeler gauge inserted between the tappet head and push-rod.

Further rotate the engine in its normal direction of rotation until the exhaust tappet clearance is reduced to *nil* without causing the exhaust valve to lift. Then check and if necessary adjust the *inlet* tappet clearance using the same procedure as for the exhaust tappet.

On O.H.V.s (B31–B34, M33) it is best, when checking the tappet clearance with a feeler gauge, to take the weight of the push-rod off the tappet by lifting the push-rod with the fingers. This facilitates proper entry of the feeler gauge and accurate checking of the valve clearance.

Referring to Fig. 37, to adjust the tappet clearance, with the appropriate tappet spanner, loosen the lock-nut *B* while holding the tappet head *A* with another spanner. Then prevent the tappet from rotating by holding it with a spanner applied to the flat on the tappet stem *C* and screw the tappet adjusting nut *A* (i.e. the tappet head) up or down as required to decrease or increase the clearance respectively. When the correct tappet clearance has been obtained, tighten lock-nut *B* firmly against the adjusting nut *A*, without moving the latter. If the lock-nut is at all stiff on the tappet stem thread, hold the tappet with a spanner applied to the flat on the stem until nuts *A* and *B* are in contact. Before replacing the tappet cover and washer, again check the clearances with a feeler gauge.

Exhaust-Valve Lifter Adjuster (B31–B34, M33). On the 350 c.c., 500 c.c. O.H.V. engines (B31–B34, M33) the exhaust-valve lifter cam (Fig. 38) must be kept well clear of the rocker arm inside the exhaust rocker-box. Failure to maintain adequate exhaust-valve lifter clearance upsets tappet clearance, occasions mechanical noise, and worse still, causes a tendency for the exhaust valve to burn up. On the 350 c.c., 500 c.c. O.H.V. engines, effect exhaust-valve lifter adjustment by the cable adjuster screwed into the exhaust rocker-box cover. An additional adjustment on these engines can be made by removing and altering the position of the actuating lever on the serrated cam spindle.

Adjustment—Models B40, B40 SS90. Remove the sparking plug so that the engine can be readily rotated by hand with the kick-starter. Also unscrew and remove the three inspection caps from the rocker-box so as to expose push-rods and rocker adjusters. Turn the engine forward until the inlet valve has just closed and check and if necessary adjust the exhaust valve clearance. Slide a 0·008 in. feeler gauge between the end of the valve and the overhead rocker adjuster as shown in Fig. 39. If the exhaust valve clearance is incorrect loosen lock-nut *A* and with another spanner turn

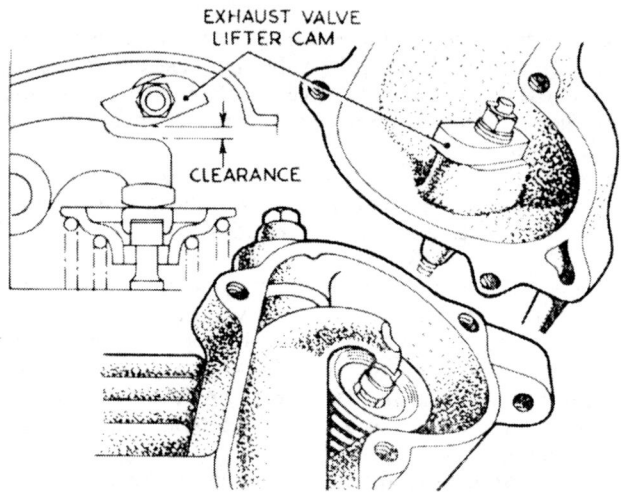

FIG. 38. EXHAUST-VALVE LIFTER ADJUSTMENT ON B.S.A. 350 C.C., 500 C.C. O.H.V. ENGINES (B31–B34, M33)

Position cam correctly on fitting rocker cover. Check split-pin.

the adjuster *B* until the feeler gauge just slides between the valve and the adjuster. Afterwards firmly re-tighten the lock-nut *A* and again check the valve clearance. Now proceed to check and if necessary adjust the inlet valve clearance.

Turn the engine forward again until the exhaust valve clearance is eliminated but before the valve begins to open. Then check and if necessary adjust the inlet valve clearance, using a 0·010 in. feeler gauge, as previously described for the exhaust valve. Having checked and if necessary adjusted the clearances for both valves, replace the sparking plug and the three inspection caps. Be careful not to damage the circular washers.

DECARBONIZING AND VALVE GRINDING

Generally speaking, the removal of carbon deposits is necessary only when the engine displays a tendency to run hot, and when certain characteristic symptoms (*see* below) become manifest. Under normal running conditions decarbonizing should only be undertaken at periods exceeding 5,000 miles, and not till the engine *really needs it*. Valve grinding can be conveniently done when decarbonizing, and the valves and their seats should be inspected. Certain items required for the complete maintenance operation are mentioned on page 51.

The cylinder barrel should also be removed if it is felt that the piston rings should be inspected. An inspection of the piston rings is advisable

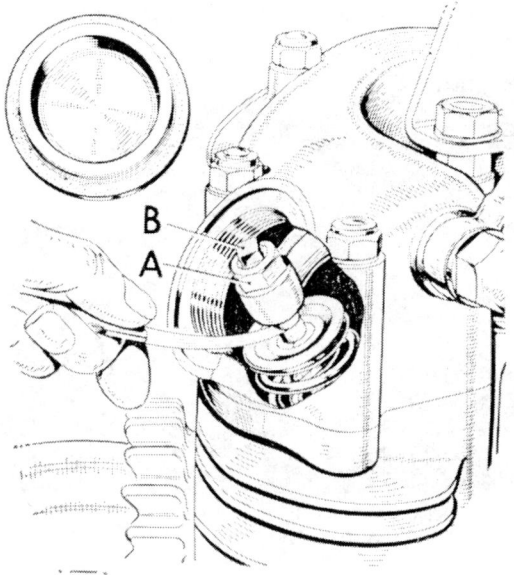

FIG. 39. CHECKING THE EXHAUST VALVE CLEARANCE
(1961–6 MODELS B40, B40 SS90)

where engine compression is poor (in spite of valve condition being good), and where there is a tendency for blue smoke to issue from the exhaust. Decarbonizing is very simple, and it is not necessary to remove the cylinder barrel during each "top overhaul" because most of the carbon deposits form on the piston crown, which is accessible on removing the cylinder head. The necessity for decarbonizing is indicated by a gradual falling off in power (especially on hills), a tendency for "pinking" (injurious to the engine) under slight provocation, and a "woolly" exhaust. The sparking plug also tends to become dirty very quickly.

Removal of the Petrol Tank (Models B31–B34, M33). Turn off the petrol and detach the petrol pipe. Then remove the two nuts and detach the strap positioned beneath the front end of the tank. Pull off the rubber grommet which conceals the tank central securing-bolt, and with a box spanner and tommy-bar remove the bolt. The petrol tank can then be withdrawn as shown in Fig. 40.

Removing Petrol Tank (Models B40, B40 SS90). Tank removal is facilitated by first removing the dualseat which is secured to the frame by the two top bolts of the rear suspension units and clipped to a cross tube at the front. Turn off the petrol tap and remove the petrol pipe after unscrewing the banjo bolt and union nuts from the carburettor and tank.

Fig. 40. Removing Quickly-detachable Petrol Tank
Fitted to Models B31–B34, M33

The petrol tank is mounted on rubber pads and secured by a single bolt. This bolt passes through a rubber sleeve in the centre of the tank to its anchorage on the frame. Remove the rubber cap on top of the tank, unscrew the nut, and withdraw the tank complete with rubber sleeve, leaving the bolt attached to the frame.

Preliminary Dismantling (Models B31–34, M33). It is assumed the petrol tank has already been removed. Next detach the h.t. lead at the plug and remove the latter. Also disconnect the steady-stay (a plate) from the frame to the rear of the cylinder head. Unscrew the ring nut on top of the carburettor mixing chamber and withdraw the carburettor slides and place them out of the way. Then remove the Amal carburettor as a unit, after removing the two flange securing-nuts. Be careful not to damage the flange washer. Also remove the exhaust system after removing the nuts securing the pipe and silencer clips to the frame. The pipe is a push fit in the exhaust port. It may be necessary to tap it carefully (avoid denting) with a mallet.

The engine is now in exactly the condition shown in Fig. 41. On 1958-60 models there is, of course, no "Magdyno" fitted.

FIG. 41. DISMANTLING B31-B34, M33 ENGINE FOR
DECARBONIZING—STAGE 1

A 1954 B31 engine is shown, but the general dismantling procedure applies to all
1955-60 B31-B34, M33 engines.

KEY

1. Support for tank (omitted for 1955-60)
2. Plug terminal cover and h.t. lead (detached)
3. Hole for plug (removed)
4. Engine steady-stay (disconnected). Plate fitted, 1955-60
5. Mixing chamber ring nut (removed from carburettor)
6. Carburettor slides (tucked away)
7. Flange for carburettor (removed)
8. Exhaust port (pipe and silencer removed altogether)
9. Unions for rocker-spindle oil feed pipe. Central feed, 1955-60
10. Union for rocker-box oil return pipe (omitted, 1955-60)

Preliminary Dismantling (Models B40, B40 SS90). Remove the petrol tank. Disconnect exhaust-valve lifter cable; and the engine steady bracket from the frame top tube. Note the order of assembly of the nuts and washers. Unscrew the ring nut on top of the carburettor and withdraw the carburettor slides and place them out of the way. On later B40 models and all B40 SS90 models remove the air filter cover to expose the filter which is retained by a spring clip. Move this aside and unscrew the adaptor sleeve from the carburettor. Now remove the Amal carburettor as a unit after removing the two nuts which secure its flange to the cylinder head flange. Slacken the nuts which hold the exhaust system to the frame and withdraw the exhaust pipe which is a push fit in the exhaust port. If necessary tap it gently with a mallet. Finally remove the sparking plug and the oil feed pipe to the overhead rocker spindles.

Removing the Cylinder Head (Models B31, B32, B33, B34, M33). After preliminary dismantling as described on page 68, disconnect the oil-feed pipe from the overhead rocker spindles and also the return pipe from the rocker-box to the crankcase. When re-assembling, it should be noted that the union screws for the oil-feed pipe to the rockers have a much smaller hole in the side than is the case with the union screw for the return pipe (fitted to 1955–7 models).

Prior to further dismantling, position the piston at T.D.C. (both valves closed) so as to free the valves from pressure.

Next disconnect the exhaust-valve lifter cable at the rocker-box,* or alternatively remove the exhaust rocker-box cover with exhaust-valve lifter cable attached. Then remove also the inlet rocker-box cover. With the "C" spanner provided in the tool-kit loosen the castellated gland-nut which holds the tapered push-rod cover to the cylinder head. Also detach the tappet inspection-plate situated at the foot of the cover, and remove the two acorn nuts which clamp the cover base to the crankcase.

With a spanner applied to the smaller (the top one) of the two hexagons, unscrew clockwise (plan view) the four long bolts which secure the cylinder head and cylinder barrel to the crankcase. Except where it is necessary to renew a holding-down bolt and socket, do not interfere with the larger hexagon used to screw the bolt socket into the crankcase. The engine is now exactly as shown in Fig. 42.

Raise the cylinder head together with the long push-rod cover, lift the push-rods off the tappets, and lower the two rods down to the crankcase face. Then raise the cylinder head and push-rod cover upward and forward until they are both clear of the cylinder barrel. No gasket is used for the cylinder-head joint, and if the joint is stiff, free the head by a few light taps with a wooden mallet, applied under the exhaust port. Finally detach the long push-rod cover from the cylinder head, keeping it square during removal. Examine the rubber oil seal.

Now to inspect the valves and their seatings it is, of course, necessary to

* The exhaust-valve lifter spring is strong, and to free the cable from the rocker-box it is advisable first to slacken the cable right off and release the nipple from the handlebar lever.

FIG. 42. DISMANTLING B31–B34, M33 ENGINE FOR
DECARBONIZING—STAGE 2

The B31 engine shown has already been dealt with as indicated (items 1–8 in Fig. 41)
Note that the gland nut 5 must be unscrewed only a few turns, not fully as shown for
photographic purposes.

KEY TO FIG. 42

1. Rocker oil-feed pipe disconnected
2. Rocker-box oil return pipe (omitted, 1955–60) disconnected
3. Exhaust-valve lifter cable disconnected
4. Inlet rocker-box (cover removed)
5. Push-rod cover gland-nut unscrewed
6. Tappet chest (inspection cover removed)
7. Stud (two) for acorn nuts (removed) securing the push-rod cover
8. Four long bolts (top hexagons unscrewed fully) securing cylinder head and barrel

remove the valves from the cylinder head. The combustion chamber must be thoroughly decarbonized (*see* page 76).

Removing the Cylinder Barrel (Models B31, B32, B33, B34, M33). Lift the cylinder barrel upward and forward into the front angle of the frame and as the piston emerges, steady the piston, and cover up the crankcase hole to prevent dirt getting into the crankcase.

Removing Cylinder Head (Models B40, B40 SS90). On these 1961–6 models long studs secure the rocker-box to the cylinder head and it is

FIG. 43. REMOVING CYLINDER HEAD AND PUSH-ROD COVER TOGETHER
(MODELS B31–B34, M33)

When doing this, first lower the push-rods (not shown) on to the crankcase face. It is possible to remove the head and the cover separately, but this is not advised because it is likely to damage the rubber oil seal between the head and the cover.

therefore necessary to remove the rocker-box and cylinder head *together*. The cylinder head itself is secured to the cylinder barrel by 4 or 6 studs which pass through the cylinder fins into the crankcase. To remove the cylinder head, proceed as follows. First position the piston at top dead centre on the compression stroke (both valves closed) so as to free the valves from pressure. Do not disturb the rocker-box.

Remove the 4 or 6 nuts from the studs securing the cylinder head and barrel, after the preliminary dismantling referred to on page 69 has been completed. Then raise the cylinder head sufficiently to clear the crankcase studs. Turn the cylinder-head/rocker-box assembly about the inlet and exhaust push-rods until the assembly clears the top tube of the frame. Then lift the assembly, complete with rocker-box and push-rods, off the cylinder barrel. On all 1961–6 343 c.c. "Star" engines the push-rods operate in a tunnel cast integral with the cylinder barrel and cylinder head. Both push-rods can now be withdrawn from the cylinder-head/rocker-box assembly and should be marked to ensure correct identification. To give access to the valves the rocker-box can now be removed. Examine the cylinder head gasket carefully. Both sides should be clean and bright. A new gasket is required if any dark patches are found on either surface.

Removing the Cylinder Barrel (Models B40, B40 SS90). It is undesirable to remove the cylinder barrel from the crankcase unless lack of compression (with the valves in good condition) and the presence of excessive blue

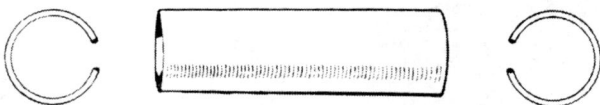

FIG. 44. GUDGEON-PIN AND CIRCLIPS
Note that the circlips have plain ends.

moke in the exhaust indicate that the piston rings need attention. Prior to removing the cylinder barrel rotate the engine to get piston at B.D.C. Slacken the two crankcase nuts at the base of the cylinder flange. Then gently ease the cylinder barrel off the piston until the latter emerges from the barrel. As it does so steady the piston to prevent its coming into sharp contact with the crankcase mouth. Cover the top of the crankcase with a piece of clean rag to prevent the entry of foreign matter.

Piston Removal. The piston (removal seldom needed) is of aluminium alloy with two compression rings and one slotted scraper ring (Fig. 45). It is held to the small-end of the connecting-rod by a fully floating gudgeon-pin, secured to the piston by circlips (*see* Fig. 44). The gudgeon-pin is a close fit in the piston when the latter is cold. To remove it safely, *first warm the piston* by laying an electric iron on its crown, or by applying a rag immersed in boiling water and wrung out. Then press out the pin after circlip removal.

The gudgeon-pin may be pressed out with a gudgeon-pin extractor tool (*see* Fig. 50), or tapped out with a light hammer and soft-nosed punch. Where a piston has had considerable service, it may be possible to push the pin out by hand, provided that the piston is reasonably warm.

Remove the circlips with a small screwdriver or pointed instrument such as the tang end of a ground file. Then press or tap the gudgeon-pin out from one side, supporting the piston if tapping the pin out. A circlip must fit snugly into its groove in the piston boss because if it works loose, it may ruin the cylinder. Whatever the condition of a circlip, renew it with a genuine B.S.A. one. On removing the gudgeon-pin, make a slight nick on one end to ensure correct replacement.

Marking the Piston. A piston laps out the cylinder in a certain manner depending upon piston thrust, lubrication and other factors, and it is

 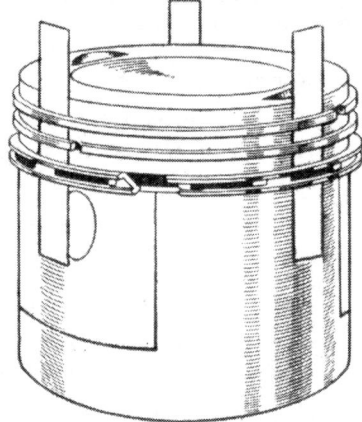

FIG. 45. PISTON AND SAFE METHOD OF REMOVING RINGS

This method (see text) should also be used for refitting rings. Note the slotted scraper ring below the two compression rings. On all later type engines a split-skirt type piston is fitted. The piston shown on the left is worn, scored and blackened (rebore and oversize piston needed).

most vital not to replace it in any except its original position on the connecting-rod; it should not be replaced back to front. Therefore, unless the piston has some distinguishing characteristic it is always advisable to mark it to ensure its correct replacement. Perhaps the best plan is to scratch an "F" on the inside to indicate which is the front. Always remember that a piston should be handled with great care, as it is readily distorted or cracked. Test the connecting-rod for vertical play. None should exist, but a little side play is normal. *See* also page 124.

Examining and Removing the Piston Rings. The piston rings are the main-guard of the compression. They must, therefore, be full of spring, free in their grooves, and set with their gaps opposite to each other (i.e. at 120° in the case of a three-ring piston). If all three rings have a smooth metallic surface, they are satisfactorily contacting the cylinder bore, and are perfect, and should be left alone. If, on the other hand, they are shiny or stained at some points, they are not in good contact with the bore of the cylinder. Perhaps they are stuck in their grooves with burnt oil, but will function properly if the grooves are cleaned. If the rings are scored, or have lost their tension (minimum free gap: $\frac{3}{16}$ in.), or are vertically loose in their grooves or have brown patches, the rings must be renewed.

Piston rings are of cast-iron and, being of very small section, must be

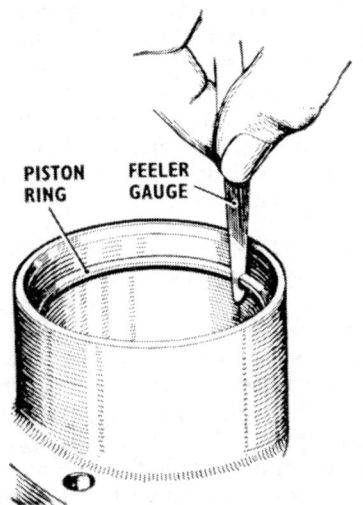

PISTON RING   FEELER GAUGE

FIG. 46. CHECKING PISTON RING GAP

handled very, very carefully. If not, they will certainly be broken. Scraper rings are particularly vulnerable; they cannot safely be opened out wider than will allow them to slip over the crown of the piston. Therefore, to put them on or remove them requires the insertion of small strips of sheet-metal, about $\frac{1}{2}$ in. wide by 2 in. long, which are placed in the manner shown in Fig. 45. Be most careful to note the order in which the rings are removed so as to ensure proper replacement. When fitting piston rings, thoroughly clean the grooves into which they fit, as any deposit left at the back of new rings forces them out and makes them too tight a fit. Paraffin usually loosens stuck piston rings.

Piston rings are made to very accurate dimensions, and it is very bad practice to attempt to "fit" oversize or undersize rings unless you know exactly what you are doing. Lapping-in oversize piston rings is a skilful job, and unless the slot sizes are exactly right, the rings will not function well, and may even produce an engine seizure. Therefore, always use piston rings supplied by B.S.A. Motor Cycles, Ltd. The gap for all new rings should not be less than 0·009 in. or exceed 0·013 in. (all engines). Test the gap occasionally with feeler gauges and if it exceeds 0·024 in. fit a new ring (if barrel wear is not excessive). Check its gap. When testing the ring gap, insert the ring into the least worn part of cylinder bore and slide up the piston so that its top locates the ring squarely.

Keep an eye on the ends of the three rings. If they are bright, this indicates that the gap is insufficient; if, on the other hand, they are thick with carbon the gap is probably excessive. If the gap of a new ring is less than 0·009 in. clamp the ring between two wood blocks in a vice and file one of the diagonal ends slightly. If a new ring is found to be a tight fit in its groove, rub down one side of the ring on a piece of carborundum paper laid on a sheet of plate glass. A slotted scraper ring is fitted on B.S.A. pistons (Fig. 45) and this can usually be fitted either way up.* All three rings should be assembled in the manner shown in Fig. 45. A final word of advice: if the piston is doing its job well, leave the rings alone. Good compression indicates that all is well.

Removing the Carbon. Thoroughness in decarbonizing well repays the labour expended. To clean the cylinder head, the best tool is a proprietary scraper, blunt knife, or screwdriver, with which the carbon can be scraped and chipped from the head, great care being taken to see that the combustion chamber is not deeply scratched. The author finds that a small electrical screwdriver is excellent for decarbonizing the curved inside of the combustion chamber. To avoid damaging the valve seats, always first insert the valves in their guides if these have been removed.

Remove all traces of carbon from the interior surfaces and do not forget the sparking plug hole and the exhaust port. Carbon forms less readily on a smooth surface and therefore it is a good plan to polish a cast-iron type head with fine emery cloth, but do this *before* removing the valves, and afterwards clear all abrasive particles away with paraffin. Also scrape all carbon from the valve heads. Be very careful with an aluminium-alloy head and do not use emery cloth or caustic soda on it.

In the case of an O.H.V. head with metal-to-metal joint, care should be taken that the ground joint of the head is not damaged. A good method of holding the head whilst decarbonizing is to fit a hexagon steel bar, turned and threaded at one end into the plug hole. The cylinder head may then be held in a vice by means of the steel bar. If such a bar is not available, an old sparking plug makes a useful substitute.

With a soft aluminium-alloy piston (moved to T.D.C.) be careful when removing the carbon. *Do not use emery cloth;* the carbon can be removed

---

* With a stepped or chamfered scraper ring, fit the ring with the step or chamfer uppermost. On Models B40, B40 SS90 the lower compression ring is of the tapered type. One of its faces is marked "TOP" and this ring must be fitted with this face uppermost.

by means of a proprietary scraper, a blunt knife, or blunt screwdriver, and the surface afterwards can be wiped with a rag damped in paraffin. Never attempt to remove carbon from the skirt or the lands between the rings. A little carbon is usually deposited on the *inside* of the piston. When the piston is removed, this should be removed. The screwdriver, or other scraper can be used for this until all carbon is scraped off. If the piston is not removed, do not disturb the carbon on its circumference, which forms a good oil seal. It is a good plan to place an old piston ring on top of the piston. Examine all ring grooves for carbon. Should any be present, scrape out with a tool such as that shown in Fig. 47. The rings should also be scraped at the back. Wash the piston and rings thoroughly in clean paraffin. Refit the rings by slipping them over the piston, using, if necessary, the method shown in Fig. 45.

Stripping the Cylinder Head (B31, B32, B33, B34, M33). It is not necessary when removing valves for grinding-in, to detach the overhead

END GROUND TO A VEE

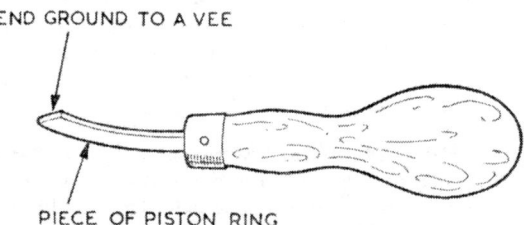

PIECE OF PISTON RING

FIG. 47. A USEFUL TOOL FOR CLEANING PISTON RING GROOVES

rockers, but if a complete strip is decided upon, proceed in the following manner. With a suitable spanner remove the acorn nuts on the rocker spindles. Then tap the spindles out, using a small centre-punch to prevent damaging the threads on the spindle ends. When dismantling, note the correct order of assembly for future attention. This is: (*a*) spring; (*b*) steel washer; (*c*) aluminium oil-seal washer.

Stripping the Cylinder Head (B40, B40 SS90). Rocker-box removal is necessary prior to valve removal. Remove the three inspection covers. Also remove the two thin nuts and washers from the steady-bracket studs, and the seven $\frac{1}{4}$ in. nuts and washers from the remaining studs. Then withdraw the rocker-box and gasket from the cylinder head. For rocker-box dismantling instructions, *see* page 123.

To Remove the Valves. As has already been mentioned (page 67) the valves should be removed and inspected when you are decarbonizing, and *if necessary* ground-in. The valves are, of course, housed in the detachable head. Split collets are used for valve-spring anchorage on all

B.S.A. engines. To remove them, it is desirable to use a good valve-spring compressor (which may be purchased from any B.S.A. dealer). This particularly applies to engines where the outer valve spring collars are awkwardly placed. Split collets often become stuck, and after turning the tommy-bar or wing nut of the compressor a few turns, loosen the split collet by delivering a sharp tap with a hammer on the forked end of the compressor. Be careful not to lose the valve-stem end caps (B31 and B32 engines). *Do not mix up inlet and exhaust collets.*

Should no valve-spring compressor be available, the following method can be employed for compressing the valve springs on all the O.H.V. engines. Place some hard packing under the valve heads; place the cylinder or cylinder head so that the valves or packing are flush with the bench. Then press down on the valve spring outer collar with a spanner or other suitable tool until the spring is compressed enough to enable the split collet to be removed. The valve can then be drawn out, and the duplex spring and collars removed. The valve springs are powerful and the author strongly advises the use of a compressor (*see* Fig. 49) for valve removal. The B.S.A. compressor (Service tool No. 84061–3340) is shown in Fig. 49.

FIG. 48.
VALVE-
GRINDING
TOOL

How to Grind-in Valves. Use the valve grinding tool* shown in Fig. 48. To grind-in a valve (see that it is the correct one), holding the cylinder or cylinder head firmly on a bench or in a vice *see* (page 76), clean both the valve seat and valve; smear, with a piece of rag or the finger tip, a thin film of fine grinding paste (coarse at first if dealing with a valve and seat in poor condition) on the valve face; replace the valve its in guide minus the valve spring. Before replacing it, however, it is a good plan to insert a light spring between the valve head and valve guide. This avoids the necessity of frequently lifting the valve off its seat, by hand, when turning it round to avoid the formation of grooves or rings on the valve face. Never interchange the inlet and exhaust valves (marked "IN" and "EX" respectively). On many engines the valves cannot be interchanged because the diameter of the exhaust-valve stem is greater than that of the inlet-valve stem.

When grinding-in, a light pressure on the grinding tool is required and care must be taken not to rock the valve, particularly if the valve guide is somewhat worn. Rotate the valve about *a third of a turn* in one direction and then an equal amount in the opposite direction, pausing every few oscillations to raise the valve from its seat and turn it one-third to a quarter of a revolution. Cease grinding-in when no "cut" can be felt (and the valve begins to "sing") and put some more paste on the bevelled

* To secure good adhesion, moisten the rubber end of B.S.A. tool 65–9240.

edge of the valve face if, after cleaning the valve in paraffin, some pitting is still visible.

Continue grinding-in until both the valve face and seat have a matt metallic surface uniformly over an appreciable width (line contact is not sufficient) and there are no pit marks left after wiping the paste off. Excessive grinding-in after a good seating has been effected eventually leads to the valves becoming "pocketed," which causes a considerable decline in power output. Take badly pitted valves or seats to a B.S.A. dealer for re-grinding and re-facing (at 45 deg.) respectively.

SPLIT COLLETS

After grinding-in the inlet and exhaust valves, wipe both the valves and their seats thoroughly clean with a paraffin- or petrol-soaked rag to ensure that there is absolutely no trace of any abrasive left. Examine the valve guides for wear and renew if much play exists, otherwise slow-running will become difficult. Often a valve stem wears more than its guide does, and a distinct shoulder is felt near the neck of the valve. In this case fitting a new valve (which must be ground-in) will probably remedy slackness without fitting a new valve guide. Also renew the valve springs if weak. If rough, smooth the ports with a riffler.

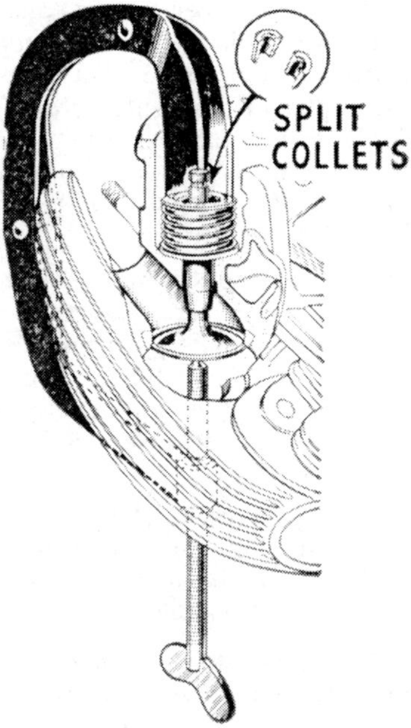

FIG. 49. THE B.S.A. VALVE-SPRING COMPRESSOR (SERVICE TOOL No. 84061–3340)

Fitting New Valve Guides. If the valve guides on an O.H.V. engine are worn badly enough to require renewal, the old guides may be driven out with tool 83261–3265 applied from inside the cylinder head. New guides must be driven in from the top as far as they can go. Note that when new valve guides are fitted it is essential to have the valve seats refaced with a proper valve seat cutter. This ensures that each seat is concentric with the bore of the corresponding valve guide. A circlip is not fitted to the valve guides on Models B40, B40 SS90.

Refitting the Valves. After grinding-in the valves you should reassemble them in the correct positions in the cylinder head.

On B31, B32 engines, do not forget to replace the hardened valve stem end-caps. Before replacing the valve springs, check that they have not lost their tension by comparing them with a new spring. Loss of tension, due mainly to heat, sometimes occurs after several thousand miles, and the free length of the valve springs is reduced. This necessitates renewal and where such renewal is, or soon will be, required, it is obviously wise to effect valve spring renewal during decarbonizing procedure.

Smear the valve stems with oil and replace them in their guides. Then refit the valve springs and collars, being careful not to mix up the upper and lower collars. Next compress each valve spring and refit the split collet, making certain that it "beds down" properly. On O.H.V. engines the application of a little grease to the inside of a split-collet enables it to facilitate reassembly. *Note*: on some engines the exhaust collet is *thinner* than the inlet. Wrong replacement can cause a valve to drop into the cylinder! On Model B40 SS90 the close coils of the valve springs should be at the bottom.

Valve Spring Renewal. Valve springs are cheap and, if shortened, may damage the valves. The correct free lengths for *new* (O.H.V.) inner and outer springs are $1\frac{13}{16}$ in. and $2\frac{5}{32}$ in. respectively for Models B31–B34 and M33. For Model B40 the correct free lengths for *new* inner and outer springs are $1\frac{5}{8}$ in. and $2\frac{1}{32}$ in. respectively. For Model B40 SS90 the correct free lengths for *new* inner and outer springs are $1\frac{1}{2}$ in. and 1·67 in. respectively.

Fitting Overhead Rockers (Models B31–34, M33). To fit each rocker, tap in the spindle and fit spring, steel washer, rocker, and aluminium washer; tap the spindle hard home and tighten the acorn nuts. *The oil groove should be uppermost.*

Grinding-in the Cylinder Head and Barrel Faces. If either face on an O.H.V. engine (with metal-to-metal joint) has been damaged in removal of the head, it will be necessary to regrind them in, in the same manner as one would a valve. The holes from which the bolts have been taken should first be filled with grease, so that the grinding compound is kept out of the threads. The head and barrel should then be ground-in.

Rebores and Oversize Pistons. Inspect the bore of the cylinder barrel closely for wear when the barrel is removed. Should a deep ridge be felt at the top end, it may be desirable to have the cylinder rebored. Take the cylinder barrel to the nearest B.S.A. dealer to get an expert opinion. The cylinder barrel will also need to be rebored if there are any deep score marks causing loss of compression and excessive oil consumption. Shiny marks on the bore surface indicate that a seizure has occurred, and the piston should be closely examined.

Note that pistons $\frac{1}{2}$ mm and 1 mm oversize are obtainable for rebore purposes. In the U.K. there is also an Exchange Replacement system enabling a rebored cylinder barrel with piston to match to be obtained from a local B.S.A. spares stockist or dealer.

Refitting the Piston and Cylinder Barrel. This should be done in the reverse order of dismantling. Smear the piston and inside of the cylinder barrel with engine oil and refit the piston on the connecting-rod the correct way round (page 74), pressing or tapping home the oiled gudgeon-pin, from one side after fitting a new circlip on the other. If the gudgeon-pin refuses to go home, warm the piston (see page 73), and do not forget to support it when using a hammer and soft-nosed drift.

FIG. 50. PRESSING THE GUDGEON-PIN HOME INTO THE PISTON WITH A
TERRY TOOL

On the stripped machine illustrated (the author's 1957 Model B31) the gudgeon-pin has been pressed nearly home into the 0·02-in. over-size Hepolite piston, after fitting a new circlip on the near side. Note the three alternative pressure pads on the ends of the tommy-bar and pressure screw. A new exhaust tappet and guide have just been fitted, and the guide is shown partly screwed home. To remove the exhaust tappet, by the way, it is necessary to remove the exhaust camwheel-spindle and also the main-shaft pinion, using B.S.A. extractors, Part Nos. 61–691 and 61–1735 respectively. The outrigger plate (*see* Fig. 52) has not yet been bolted on. If a "Magdyno" is removed, be sure to replace the original base shims.

Fit a second new circlip (even if the old one seems perfect) and see that it beds down properly in the piston-boss slot and is fully expanded. Remember that if a circlip fails while the engine is running you may have to put your hand in your pocket for a new piston and cylinder. Also see that the cylinder-barrel spigot and mouth of the crankcase are scrupulously clean and that the base washer is intact and replaced. Smear it lightly with some jointing compound (*see* page 84).

To replace the cylinder barrel, put the crank slightly past B.D.C. with tappets right down, position the ring gaps (*see* page 74), hold the cylinder barrel with both hands (or suspend it from the top-tube) over the piston; with help (or unaided), offer up the piston. The rings must be squeezed together (by hand or with slipper No. 81461-3682), and the barrel slid over the piston until the complete piston enters the cylinder. Avoid putting any side strain on the piston or connecting-rod.

On B31–B34, M33 engines the long bolts which secure the cylinder barrel and head are not, of course, raised and tightened until *after* the cylinder head has been replaced. Put piston at T.D.C.

Final Reassembly (Models B31, B32, B33, B34, M33).   Place the cover for the push-rods into position in the cylinder head; do not tighten up the gland nut. Fit the push-rods into the long cover and offer up the cylinder head (with rocker inspection-cover removed). Keep the cylinder head slightly raised while positioning the lower ends of the push-rods (not crossed) on the tappets. Then engage the upper ends of the push-rods with the overhead rockers.

Lower the cylinder head into position, replace and tighten firmly the two acorn nuts which secure the push-rod cover base and fit and screw up diagonally the four long cylinder-barrel and head securing-bolts. These bolts must be tightened firmly and evenly. Tighten securely the gland nut of the long push-rod cover, using the "C" spanner in the tool kit.

Check the tappet clearances (*see* page 64) prior to fitting the tappet and rocker inspection-covers, and adjust the clearances if necessary. Replace the cylinder head steady-stay and connect up the oil feed and return pipes to the rockers and head (test for oil flow). Tighten firmly the union screws (9) and (10) (Fig. 41).

Fit both rocker-box covers, the Amal carburettor unit, the exhaust system, and the petrol tank and pipe. On 1955–60 "swinging arm" models after positioning the quickly-detachable petrol tank (*see* Fig. 40) replace the strap at the front end of the tank and tighten evenly the two fixing nuts. Then with the box spanner and tommy-bar provided, tighten down the single bolt which secures the petrol tank to the frame top tube. Afterwards replace the rubber grommet and connect up the petrol pipe. Replace the sparking plug, which is assumed to have been dismantled, cleaned, and if necessary re-gapped.

Final Assembly (Models B40, B40 SS90).   Apply a dab of grease to the lower ends of the inlet and exhaust push-rods. Then insert the latter through the cylinder-barrel tunnel so that the *outer* tappet operates the *inlet* push-rod and the *inner* tappet the *exhaust* push-rod. The correct assembly of the push-rods is shown in Fig. 51.

Replace the cylinder head gasket on the cylinder barrel face. Fit a new gasket if there are signs of burning, particularly round the cylinder bore.

The gasket besides having four holes for the cylinder barrel studs, has four oil drainage holes. See that these holes coincide with the holes on the cylinder barrel and head faces, otherwise the oil return from the rocker-box will be obstructed. Position the piston at top dead centre on the compression stroke.

Now replace the cylinder head with the rocker-box already fitted to it, and with the push-rod inspection cover removed. This is necessary so that the inlet and exhaust push-rods can be made to engage the rocker arms as shown in Fig. 51. When replacing the cylinder head, position about 180 degrees to its normal position over the push-rods, lower it slightly, turn the head to its normal position and carefully lower the head over the 4 or 6 studs projecting through the cylinder barrel from the crankcase.

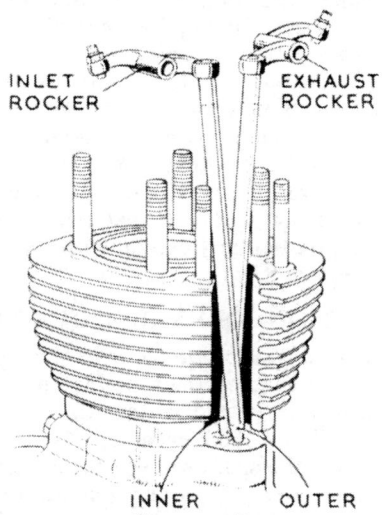

INLET ROCKER EXHAUST ROCKER

INNER OUTER

FIG. 51. SHOWING THE CORRECT POSITIONING OF THE INLET AND EXHAUST PUSH-RODS

On all B40 and B40 SS90 engines prior to engine No. B40-2479 the two smaller studs adjacent to the push-rod tunnel were omitted.

Through the inspection apertures in the rocker-box engage the cupped ends of the push-rods with the ball pins on the overhead-rocker arms. See that the outer push-rod engages the inlet rocker, and the inner push-rod the exhaust rocker as shown in Fig. 51.

Replace the 4 or 6 cylinder barrel and cylinder head retaining nuts and tighten these lightly at first and then a quarter of a turn at a time in a diagonal order. Even tightening of these nuts is very important. Replace the push-rod inspection covers, not omitting sealing washers which must be in perfect condition. Finally tighten the 2 slackened crankcase nuts.

Fit the Amal carburettor and its air filter connexion, followed by the exhaust system and engine steady bracket. When replacing the carburettor make sure that its flange washer is perfect, otherwise air leakage may occur, and tighten the two securing nuts evenly. Also when inserting the air slide be careful not to bend the throttle needle. Replace the petrol tank, connect up the petrol pipe securely to the tank and carburettor, and replace the dualseat. Finally adjust the valve clearances correctly (see page 66) and replace the sparking plug and its washer. It is assumed that the plug has been cleaned and the gap between its points set correctly (*see* page 56). Also re-connect the exhaust-valve lifter cable.

Note Concerning Gaskets. The 1955–60 B31–B34, M33 engines have a metal-to-metal cylinder-head joint and no gasket or jointing compound is necessary. Paper washers are required elsewhere (on the rocker-box cover, tappet and rocker inspection-covers, sump filter cover-plate, timing-case cover, cylinder base, etc.). To prevent oil leaks it is essential that all joint faces are absolutely clean. For cleaning up joint faces the author finds a carpenter's scraper plate very suitable.

The author advocates using jointing compound (except for the rocker and tappet inspection-cover washers, which should be greased). If a home-made timing-case cover washer is used, see that the small oil-hole is included at its base. Be particularly careful with the cylinder head gasket on 1961–6 models (see page 83).

IGNITION AND VALVE TIMING

Ignition Timing. Accurate ignition timing is extremely important. Many riders imagine that by advancing their timing they will necessarily get more speed. This is a fallacy, and it only throws unfair loads on the engine, spoiling its flexibility, and eventually damaging it throughout. For all normal road uses, the spark settings recommended by the makers should be closely adhered to. Only for genuine racing purposes is it advisable to increase the spark advance beyond these limits, and even then undue spark advance should be avoided. It should always be remembered that should the timing be so far advanced that maximum combustion pressures are reached with the crank in true T.D.C. position, the big-end comes in for a terrific hammering for which it is not designed. If a "Magdyno" has been removed for any purpose, or the drive disturbed, it will be necessary to re-time the ignition.

It is a rare occurrence on 1955–7 "Magdyno" models for the "Magdyno" sprocket to slacken off, and normally the ignition timing is best not interfered with. On all engines accurate contact-breaker gap is essential.

On 1958–66 coil ignition models with an alternator and no magneto the ignition timing rarely alters, but it is advisable to check the timing after altering the contact-breaker gap. A slight alteration in the gap affects ignition timing. Increasing the gap advances the timing and decreasing the gap retards the timing. The author's advice is: leave the timing alone if performance is good and *contact-breaker gap correct.*

Adjusting the Ignition Timing (1955–7 "Magdyno" Models B31, B32, B33, B34, M33). If adjustment is necessary, first verify that the gap between the contacts of the contact-breaker, fully open, is 0·012–0·015 in. (page 59). Next detach the timing cover. When doing this be particularly careful not to damage the small nozzle inside, which delivers pressure oil to the hollow timing-side mainshaft. As a precaution it is advisable while actually breaking the timing-cover joint to leave three equally spaced timing-cover screws in position. Half unscrew them.

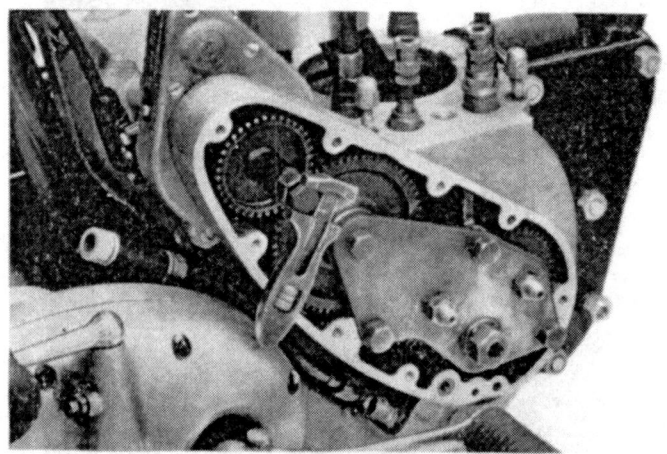

Fig. 52. Timing Cover Removed, showing "Magdyno" Driving Gear (top left) and Outrigger Plate Supporting Intermediate Gear and Both Camwheels

Applies to all "Magdyno" models (1955–7). An extractor (61/1903) and spanner are in position ready for "Magdyno" pinion withdrawal.

Having removed the timing cover, remove the locking nut which secures the "Magdyno" pinion to its armature shaft. Engage a gear and lock the rear wheel to prevent the engine turning, and then use the special B.S.A. "Magdyno" pinion extractor; screw the externally-threaded body of the extractor (Part No. 61/1903) into the pinion boss, and then turn the extractor screw *clockwise.* A few turns should immediately free the "Magdyno" pinion from the armature-shaft taper. Renew the rubber oil-seal behind the pinion, if worn.

To adjust the ignition timing, first turn the engine in the normal direction of rotation until the piston is at true T.D.C. on the compression stroke. Check the piston position with a piece of slim rod inserted through

the plug hole. Mark the rod to show true T.D.C. Scratch another mark
$\frac{7}{16}$ in. (*see* Footnote) above the first mark. Now turn the engine slowly
backwards (by engaging top gear and turning the rear wheel backwards)
until the rod has descended in the cylinder a distance equal to a little more

FIG. 53. AN ACCURATE METHOD OF CHECKING THE IGNITION TIMING
WHEN THE CYLINDER HEAD IS REMOVED

A steel scraper plate 1 (useful for cleaning joint faces) has been laid across the barrel
top face, and a vertical measurement of the piston position before T.D.C. (compression stroke) is being taken with the steel rule 2. The ignition lever is in the full-
advance position, and the contacts are beginning to break as indicated by the thin
celophane slip 3 being just released (by a gentle pull) from the contacts. The oil bath
chain-case cover need not, of course, be removed.

than the correct ignition-marking advance. Come *forward* to the exact
point of maximum ignition-advance (taking up backlash in the process).
Then move the contact-breaker in its normal direction of rotation until the
contacts are just opening (*see* Fig. 53), with the ignition lever *fully advanced*.
    With the Lucas "Magdyno" armature and engine in this position, with

* On the 1955–8 O.H.V. Model M33 and the 1956–8 O.H.V. Model B33,
the contacts should begin to open with the piston $\frac{3}{8}$ in. before T.D.C.

a box spanner and hammer, lightly tap the "Magdyno" pinion on to its plain taper. Now moderately tighten the locking nut and proceed to check the exact ignition timing, with the ignition lever fully advanced. Make quite sure that the ignition lever *is* in the *full advance position*, otherwise you will have to retime again. Frankly, the author prefers to time the ignition by the method shown in Fig. 53. A steel rule cannot lie, whereas a piece of rod inserted through the plug hole can do so in certain circumstances. If the timing is correct, firmly tighten the "Magdyno" pinion nut, again check the timing and finally replace the timing cover. Renew the rubber oil-seals and cover washer if damaged.

Adjusting the Ignition Timing (1958–60 Models B31, B33). On the coil ignition models with an alternator instead of a dynamo it is rarely necessary to check or re-adjust the ignition timing. Before checking the timing first verify that the gap between the contacts is 0·012–0·015 in. with the contacts fully open. Adjust the gap if necessary (*see* page 61).

To check the ignition timing, first remove the contact-breaker cover and also the sparking plug. Turn the engine in its normal direction of rotation until the piston is at true T.D.C. on the compression stroke (i.e. with both valves closed). Insert a piece of slim rod through the sparking-plug hole to feel the crown of the piston, and mark the T.D.C. position on the rod when slight backward and forward movement of the engine (by means of the rear wheel with top gear engaged) causes no piston movement. Keep the rod as vertical as possible. Scratch another mark on the rod $\frac{7}{16}$ in. (B31) or $\frac{3}{8}$ in. (B33) above the T.D.C. mark.

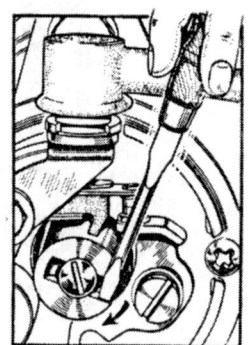

FIG. 54. MOVING CAM TO FULL ADVANCE
(Applicable to 1958–60 O.H.V. Models.)

Now turn the engine *backwards* through about 45 degrees and bring it forward again until the contacts of the contact-breaker are just beginning to open with the *ignition fully advanced*. To obtain the fully advanced position, move the cam as indicated in Fig. 54. The position of the contacts at the moment of opening is best determined by inserting a thin cellophane slip or a piece of fine paper between them and exerting a gentle pull. If the ignition timing is correct, the $\frac{7}{16}$ in. or $\frac{3}{8}$ in. mark on the rod should exactly replace the position of the T.D.C. mark with the piston at T.D.C.

Referring to Fig. 55, if the ignition timing is found to be *slightly* incorrect, loosen bolt *A* and rotate the contact-breaker a few degrees backwards or forwards as required (with the piston position correct) until the contacts are on the point of opening. Afterwards re-tighten bolt *A*.

If the ignition timing is found to be *considerably* wrong, remove the contact-breaker, complete with housing, by withdrawing the three top timing-cover screws (that at the top of the timing cover and one on each side). These three screws are longer than the other timing-cover screws which need not be removed and have nuts *B* at the back. Having withdrawn the three screws, draw out the contact-breaker, with housing, as a complete unit, together with the driving pinion which is still in position. Disconnect the l.t. cable *C* from its terminal.

Turn the engine until the piston is in the correct ignition timing position. Hold the contact-breaker unit, remove its cover, and turn the driving

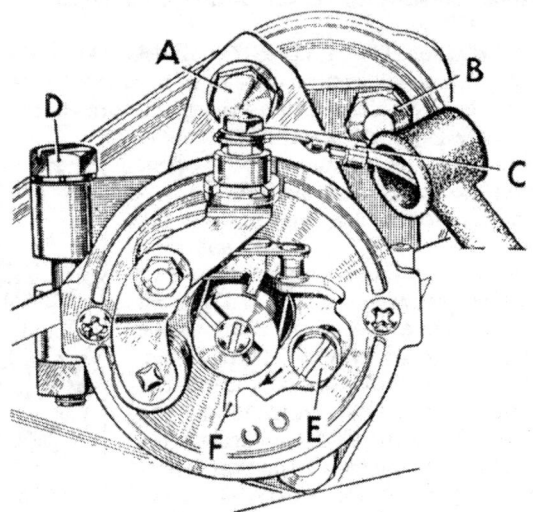

FIG. 55. THE 1958–60 CONTACT-BREAKER ASSEMBLY

pinion until the contacts are about to open with the cam held fully advanced. Release the cam and hold the unit (*see* Fig. 55) in such a position that the nut *A* and terminal *C* are vertical. If they are not in alignment, loosen the pinch bolt *D* and turn the housing until *A* comes into line with *C*. Afterwards re-tighten the pinch bolt *D*. With the unit held in this position, gently insert it into its register at the back of the timing cover. Should it fail to go right home, withdraw the unit and turn the pinion the fraction of a tooth (to permit it to mesh with the idler pinion) and position it. Replace the three timing-cover securing screws and check the ignition timing. Make any necessary adjustment by means of bolt *A*.

Ignition Timings for 1961–4 Models B40, B40 SS90. The piston position before T.D.C. on the compression stroke when the contacts of the contact-breaker commence to open varies on different engines. On Model B40 prior to engine No. 4331 and on Model B40 SS90 prior to engine No. BS1O1 the correct setting is $\frac{1}{16}$ in. before T.D.C. On Model B40 from engine No. 4331 and on Model B40 SS90 from engine No. BS1O1 the correct setting is 0·007 in. before T.D.C. All the above settings are with the ignition fully retarded, and the automatic-advance mechanism fully retards the ignition when the engine is stationary. Using a timing degree disc (*see* Fig. 56), 0·007 in. is equivalent to $33\frac{1}{2}°$ before T.D.C.

Adjusting the Ignition Timing (1961–4 Models B40, B40 SS90). First remove the sparking plug and engage top gear to enable the piston to be moved slowly by hand pressure on the rear wheel. Insert a slim rod, of sufficient length to prevent entry into the cylinder, through the sparking plug hole so that the piston position can be determined. Turn the engine over by hand pressure on the kick-starter until the piston reaches the top of its compression stroke and both valves are closed. If both valves are not closed the piston is on the wron g stroke and the engine must be turned through one more revolution. *Contact-breaker gap must be* 0·015 in.

Scratch a line on the rod level with some convenient part of the engine. Then remove the rod and scratch a further mark above the original one at a distance equal to the correct ignition timing. Replace the rod, rotate the engine backwards (to take up back-lash) by turning the rear wheel until the piston has descended an inch, and then rotate the engine forward until the upper mark on the rod rises to the same position as did the original mark. The piston is then at the correct distance before top dead centre (T.D.C.) and in this position the contacts of the contact-breaker should be just about to open. This is best determined by inserting a piece of very thin paper (such as a cigarette paper) or a celophane slip between the contacts. They will be about to open when the paper or slip can be withdrawn with a gentle pull.

If the timing is not correct with the piston positioned as described, slacken (1961–4) the clip screw shown at *E* in Fig. 58 and turn the contact-breaker housing gently until the contacts are just about to open. Re-tighten the clip screw and again check the timing, as movement of the housing may have disturbed the timing gear backlash. *See* page 124.

Valve Timing. The correct timing (*see* pages 90, 124) for the various B.S.A. engines has been determined by the manufacturers after much experiment and calculation, and B.S.A. owners are advised not to alter the original timings. All B.S.A. timing gears are marked for assembly.

Valve Timing (Models B31, B32, B33, B34, M33). On the 1955–7 350 c.c. 500 c.c. B.S.A. "Magdyno" models, removal of the timing cover cannot cause the two camwheels to be withdrawn, as these are supported by an outrigger plate (*see* Fig. 52) bolted to bosses inside the timing case. If this outrigger plate is removed and the camwheels are withdrawn, re-time in the following manner. Position the engine pinion keyway uppermost. Replace the inlet camwheel so that the dash mark etched between two teeth of the camwheel registers with the dash mark etched on the crankshaft pinion. Similarly replace the exhaust camwheel so that the dot between two teeth of the camwheel registers with the dot on the crankshaft pinion. The timing *must* then be correct.

Note that the timing marks are duplicated on both camwheels, because the cams are interchangeable. The dash mark must be used only for the inlet valve timing, and the dot mark for the timing of the exhaust valve.

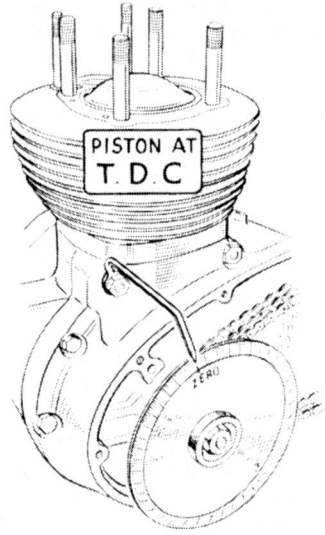

FIG. 56. DEGREE DISC AND POINTER POSITIONED FOR ACCURATELY CHECKING VALVE TIMING
Ignition timing can be checked similarly. *See* also Fig. 53.

Absolutely correct valve timing is essential, and it is even more important than precise ignition timing. On 1955–60 Models B31–B34, M33 the correct valve timing is: I.O and E.C. 25° before and after T.D.C. respectively; E.O. and I.C. 65° before and after B.D.C. respectively. The valve timing can, accurately be checked by attaching a degree disc to the crankshaft and noting the exact valve openings and closings, but this should ordinarily be quite unnecessary if the timing gears are always replaced so that their timing dash or dot marks register.

Valve Timing (1961-4 B40, B40 SS90). Disturbance of the valve timing is unlikely because the camshaft is gear driven and the timing gears are keyed to their shafts. Rarely is it necessary to dismantle the gear train.

Note that dismantling the timing case necessarily disturbs the ignition timing and it is necessary to re-time the ignition afterwards.

To obtain access to the timing gears both the outer and inner covers must be removed. To remove the outer cover first remove the exhaust system and then the gear-change and kick-starter pedals. The exhaust pipe is a push fit in the exhaust port and to free it it may be necessary to deliver a sharp blow with a soft mallet. The gear-change pedal is secured to its shaft by serrations and a clip bolt. To remove the gear-change pedal remove its securing nut and drive out the cotter pin. Now remove the outer cover after withdrawing its seven securing screws. These screws

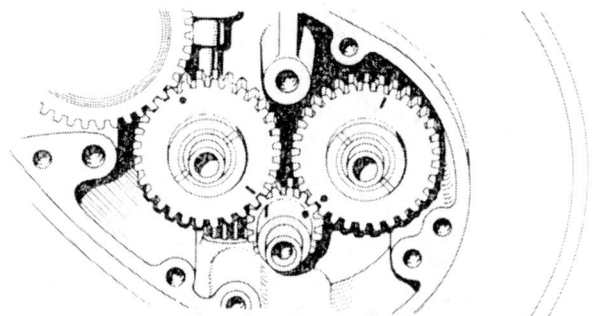

FIG. 57. TIMING-CASE COVER AND OUTRIGGER PLATE
REMOVED (1955–7 "MAGDYNO" MODELS)

Showing dash (inlet) and dot (exhaust) marks aligned for correct valve timing. *See also* Fig. 52.

have recessed heads and require a special screwdriver for removal. Note that the rearmost of the two screws at the top of the cover, shown at *E* in Fig. 58, clamps the contact-breaker unit and its removal involves re-timing the ignition after the outer cover has been replaced. *See* also page 89.

Next proceed to remove the inner cover. Disconnect the clutch cable by depressing the lever, lifting the nipple out of its slot, and withdrawing the cable and its adaptor from the rear of the cover. Care must be taken to see that the small ball located in the thrust button on the clutch actuating lever is not lost. Prise the kick-starter spring lock-plate off its locating flats on the spindle, thereby freeing both the spring and lock-plate. Remove the camshaft nut which is locked by means of a tab washer and then remove the thrust washer and locating peg.

Remove the cover plate adjacent to the gear-change spindle (secured by two screws) and withdraw the split pin from the cam plate pivot and take out the latter rearwards, leaving the cam plate inside the gearbox. Withdraw the inner cover after removing the eight screws which have recessed heads. Take great care when withdrawing the inner cover. Ease the cover off so that the camplate is not disturbed, and simultaneously apply thumb pressure to the spindle ends to retain them in their normal positions. The timing gears are now exposed as shown in Fig. 58. Note the single timing mark on each gear. Provided these marks register as shown, the valve timing must be correct. After replacing the gearbox

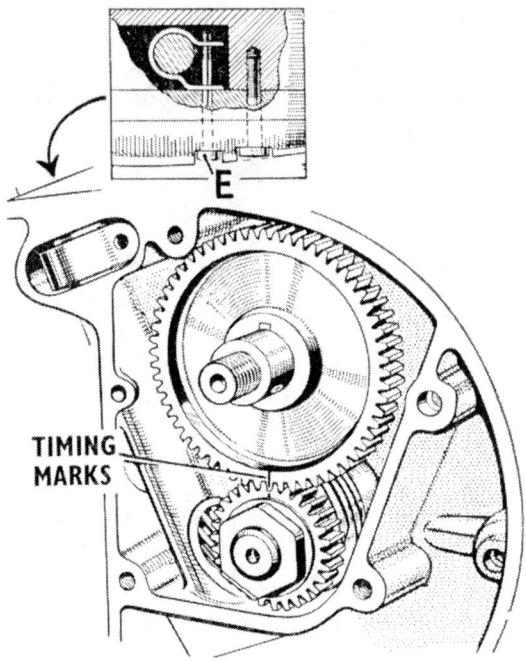

FIG. 58. VALVE TIMING MARKS ON 1961–6 MODELS B40, B40 SS90

inner and outer covers do not forget to replenish the gearbox with engine oil (*see* page 43) and to check and if necessary adjust the ignition timing (*see* page 89). For further 1961–6 valve timing data, *see* page 124.

CARE OF TRANSMISSION

Clutch Adjustment (Models With Plunger Type Rear Suspension). To prevent clutch slip or drag, it is essential to keep the clutch properly adjusted. Check the adjustment about every 2,000 miles. Referring to Fig. 59, it will be noted that the main clutch adjustment is completely enclosed in the outer cover of the gearbox. In order to make an adjustment it is therefore necessary first to unscrew the gearbox knurled filler-plug.

To effect a main adjustment of the clutch, slacken the lock-nut *A* and then, with a suitable screwdriver, turn the adjusting pin *B* until the external lever on the gearbox cover is *at right angles* to the clutch push-rod (with clutch fully disengaged). This ensures the minimum side-thrust being imposed. Afterwards tighten the lock-nut *A* and fit and tighten the filler plug. When tightening the locknut be careful not to turn the pin also.

Now make a clutch operating-cable adjustment, by means of the knurled thumb-nut *C* which is positioned on the gearbox as illustrated.

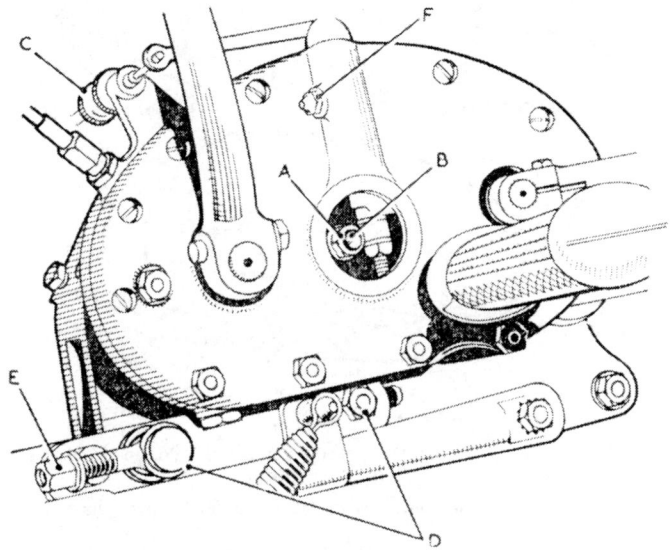

FIG. 59. CLUTCH AND PRIMARY CHAIN ADJUSTMENT ON MODELS WITH PLUNGER TYPE REAR SUSPENSION

Final adjustment of the clutch must always be made such that there is a little backlash in the clutch control cable. Absence of backlash causes the clutch to slip and subjects the plates to undue wear and tear. On the other hand, excessive backlash may give rise to clutch drag and general inefficiency. There should always be about ⅛ in. free movement of the clutch control cable at the handlebar end. The clearance decreases as the friction inserts wear.

Clutch Adjustment (Pre–1961 "Swinging Arm" Models). There must always be about ⅛ in. free movement of the clutch control cable at the handlebar end and the adjustment provided is shown in Fig. 68. To make an adjustment, remove the filler plug, loosen the lock-nut (*G*), and turn the small screw (*H*) until the long operating-lever is at right-angles to the clutch push-rod. Afterwards tighten the lock-nut securely. A cable adjustment should then be made with the knurled thumb-nut (*E*). Instructions for adjusting the clutch spring pressure are on page 95.

Clutch Adjustment (1961–4 Models B40, B40 SS90). On the 1961–4 models the main clutch adjustment is situated in the centre of the clutch

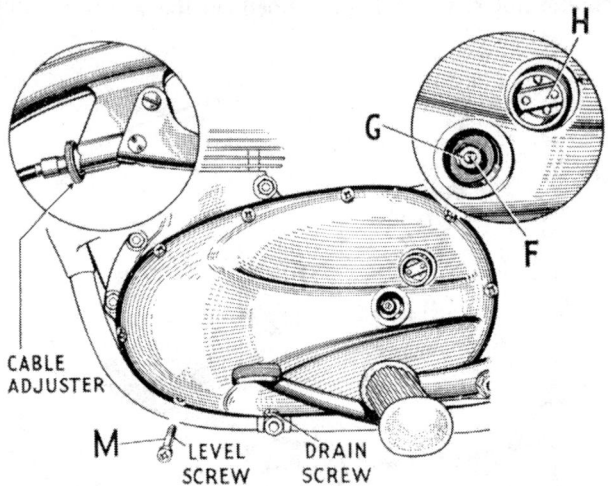

FIG. 60. THE OIL-BATH CHAIN CASE ON 1961–6 MODELS
B40, B40 SS90
Showing provision for primary chain lubrication and clutch adjustment.

pressure plate on the nearside of the engine. A cable adjuster is also provided near the clutch lever on the handlebars. There must always be $\frac{1}{16}$ in.–$\frac{1}{8}$ in. free movement of the clutch control cable at the handlebar end. To make a clutch adjustment, referring to Fig. 60, slacken off the cable adjuster near the clutch lever and remove the inspection cover *H* from the oil-bath chain case. Then loosen the lock-nut *G* and with a screwdriver screw in the adjuster *F* until all free motion is just taken up. Do not use force, otherwise the clutch plates may be separated. Now unscrew the adjuster half a turn to restore the normal working clearance. This will automatically give a little play at the handlebar lever. Then firmly tighten the lock-nut *G* and replace the inspection cover *H*. Finally adjust the handlebar-cable fine adjuster by hand as required. *See* page 120.

Increasing the Clutch Spring Pressure (1955–7). After many miles have been covered, wear of the clutch inserts may necessitate an adjustment of the clutch-spring tension being made. To make this adjustment, first expose the plates by removing the near-side footrest and the primary chain-case cover (*see* Fig. 28). Note (*see* Fig. 61) that six springs

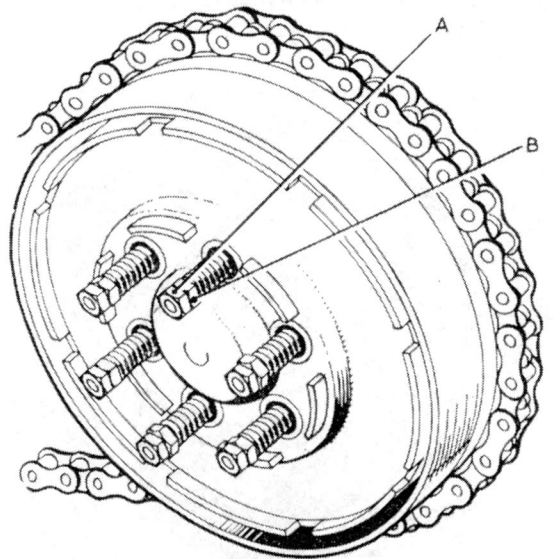

FIG. 61. ADJUSTMENT OF B.S.A. CLUTCH SPRING TENSION
(1955–7 "B" AND "M" MODELS)

are provided to keep the clutch plates pressed together. Loosen with a box spanner each of the lock-nuts *A*, while holding the nuts *B* stationary with another spanner, and then, to increase the spring tension, tighten each of the adjusting nuts *B* (clockwise) 1–2 turns. To maintain true alignment of the clutch plates, and to prevent clutch drag, it is most important to tighten all six adjusting nuts *B*, *the same number of turns.* Having made the required adjustment, tighten the six lock-nuts *A* and replace the outer half of the chain case and the near-side footrest. Finally test the clutch by disengaging it and spinning the driving plates with the kick-starter. The outer plate must turn parallel with the other plates. Also test the pressure required to operate the handlebar clutch lever.

Clutch Spring Adjustment (1958–60 Models). A simplified type of clutch assembly is provided on 1958–60 models with coil ignition. If a clutch spring adjustment is required, first remove the outer cover from the oil-bath chain case. To do this it is necessary to remove the near-side footrest and the fifteen cover-securing screws. Then to increase the spring pressure slightly (only necessary after a considerable mileage), screw in the adjusters *A* (*see* Fig. 62) *one or two turns*. To make sure that the clutch end-plate does not tilt and that the clutch frees properly, operate the clutch by means of the handlebar lever. Should the end-plate tilt, the clutch will not free properly. The remedy is to re-adjust the nuts

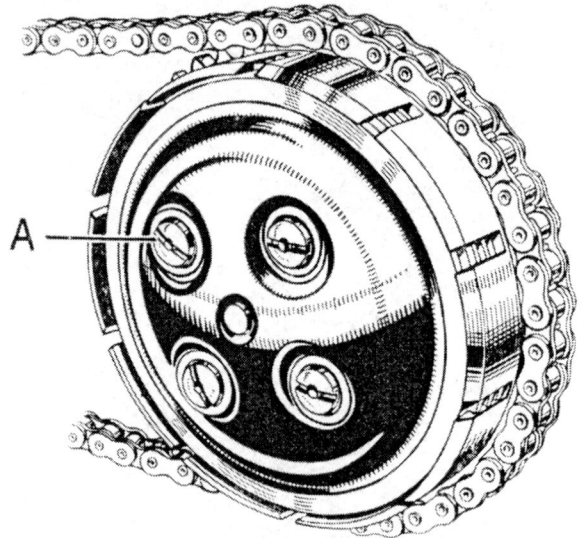

FIG. 62. ADJUSTMENT OF B.S.A. CLUTCH SPRING TENSION

Applicable to 1958–60 "B" Models. The spring adjusters have no lock-nut as on the 1955–7 clutch.

retaining the springs until the end-plate remains square when the clutch is disengaged.

Clutch Spring Adjustment (1961–6 Models B40, B40 SS90). After a considerable mileage wear of the clutch inserts may necessitate an adjustment being made to eliminate the tendency for clutch slip. An adjustment is necessary also after dismantling the clutch for any reason. It is important not to tighten the clutch springs excessively, otherwise the clutch lever will be stiff to operate and tiring to the hands.

When a clutch spring adjustment is required the cover or outer half of the oil-bath chain case must be removed. To do this first remove the near-side footrest which is fitted to a taper shaft. After removing the footrest securing nut deliver a sharp blow to free the footrest. Note that the securing nut has a left-hand thread and must be turned *clockwise* to remove. Place a suitable receptacle beneath the oil-bath chain case to catch oil as it drips out, remove all 10 screws from round the edge of the case, depress the rear brake pedal, and withdraw the cover.

Having removed the outer half of the oil-bath chaie case, the spring pressure should be adjusted carefully. The four spring sleeve-nuts shown at *P* in Fig. 63 are individually adjustable and normally each nut should be screwed in until the underside of the head is approximately $\frac{1}{8}$ in. from the face of the spring cup. This applies to plates with unworn inserts. Where wear has occurred a slightly different adjustment may be required.

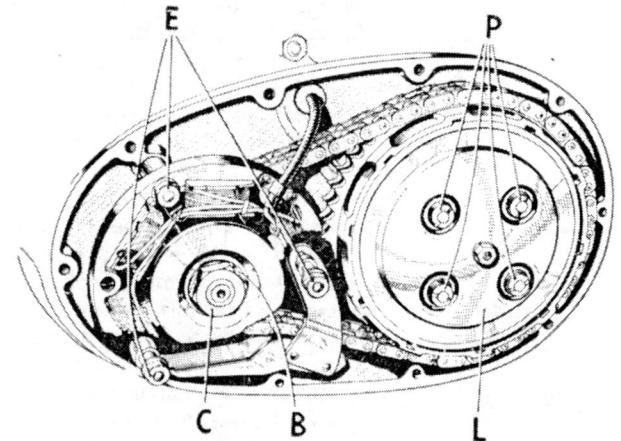

FIG. 63. OIL-BATH CHAIN CASE WITH COVER REMOVED (1961–6)
Showing clutch spring adjusters and primary chain tensioner.

It is, of course, important to tighten all the sleeve nuts the same amount. After making an adjustment verify that the clutch plates run parallel with each other when the clutch is disengaged, otherwise clutch drag and noisy gear engagement may ensue. Depress the clutch lever and operate the kick-starter. It can then be observed whether the spring pressure-plate rotates truly. If it does not, adjust the sleeve nuts individually until true running is obtained and the clutch is easy to operate.

To Dismantle the Clutch (1955–7). After a big mileage some oil may get on to the friction inserts of the clutch plates, or the inserts may be so worn that the clutch slips in spite of the adjustment of the clutch being correct. The remedy is to dismantle the clutch and clean the plates thoroughly with petrol, or get the friction plates relined, according to the state of affairs revealed when the plates are removed for inspection. Badly scored metal plates should be renewed, and the ball bearings for the clutch sprocket-plate must be in good condition.

It is desirable to inspect the central cage and the clutch-sprocket interior for burrs which can prevent the clutch plates sliding freely. Such burrs can generally be removed with a smooth file. On a machine which has done a big mileage the clutch-sprocket teeth should also be inspected. Worn teeth will cause rapid chain wear.

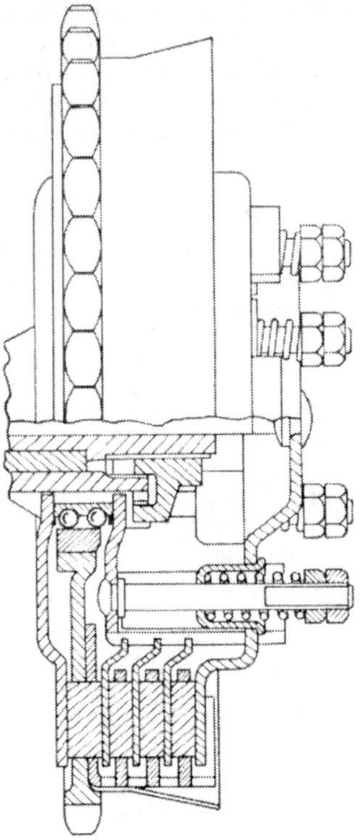

To dismantle the clutch (*see* Fig. 65), take off the near-side footrest and remove the outer cover of the oil-bath chain case. Next remove the six lock-nuts and spring adjuster-nuts (16) on the outside of the clutch pressure plate (13), and withdraw the springs (15) and the spring cups (14). Take off the clutch pressure-plate. This exposes the gearbox mainshaft nut (5) holding the clutch body (3) and clutch centre which is keyed to the main-shaft. Flatten the turned-over edge of the main-shaft-nut locking washer (4), and remove the nut (5). Then remove the complete B.S.A. clutch assembly, including the two caged ball-bearings (with one-piece inner races) from the keyed and splined clutch centre.*

During the dismantling, take careful note of the positions of the various plates and washers, to ensure correct re-assembly. As may be seen in Figs. 64, 65, plain metal plates (with tongues on the inside diameter) and Ferodo-insert plates are fitted alternately. Note that the clutch-sprocket plate on Model B31 has cork inserts, instead of the Ferodo inserts fitted to the remaining friction plates. On all other "B" and "M" models *all* inserts are of Ferodo.

FIG. 64. PARTLY-SECTIONED VIEW OF B.S.A. CLUTCH ASSEMBLY (1955-7)

On certain models two extra plates are provided, but the general layout is the same for all 1955-7 models. It applies also to 1958 "M" Models.

When reassembling the clutch, fit the key to the mainshaft if this has been removed; tap home the clutch centre, complete with back plate, fit the two ball-bearings to the clutch centre (with unbroken cage-flanges wide apart), and replace the sprocket plate. Fit the studded clutch body, and then the locking washer and the mainshaft nut. Tighten this very firmly

* The splined clutch centre is a sleeve keyed to the mainshaft taper. To remove it, use an extractor (B.S.A. Part No. 61-3362). Do not forget to fit the key when replacing the sleeve.

with a box spanner. Afterwards with a stout screwdriver (a centre-punch is not suitable) and hammer, turn over the edge of the locking washer on to the face of the nut so as to lock it. *This is most important.* It will be observed at this stage that the clutch sprocket plate has some end movement and a "rock" of about one-sixteenth of an inch (bearing maximum

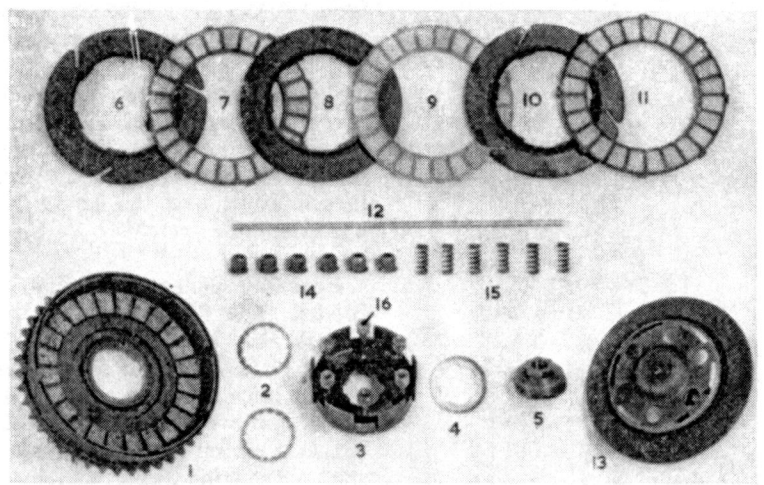

FIG. 65. THE B.S.A. CLUTCH DISMANTLED (1955–7)

The back plate on the keyed clutch centre is shown in position in Fig. 53. The remaining parts shown above are assembled in the sequence indicated by the numbers. Note particularly that the edge of the locking washer 4 must be hammered over the face of the retaining nut 5.

KEY TO FIG. 65

1. Clutch sprocket (B31) with cork inserts
2. Ball bearings for sprocket (inner races not shown)
3. Clutch body
4. Locking washer for nut 5
5. Nut securing sprocket and clutch centre
6, 8, 10. Steel (driven) plates

7, 9, 11. Friction plates (Ferodo inserts)
12. Clutch push-rod
13. Pressure plate carrying springs
14. Spring cups
15. Clutch springs (six)
16. Spring adjuster-nuts and lock-nuts

diametrical-play: 0·0015 in.). *This is quite normal.* Now fit the remaining plates (*see* Fig. 65).

When the pressure plate is replaced, smear a little grease on its centre against which the clutch push-rod bears, and see that the spring adjuster nuts are tightened evenly (*see* page 94).

To Dismantle Clutch (1958–60). On the 1958–60 "B" models it is quite simple to dismantle the clutch after removing the oil-bath chain case cover. Remove the four nuts *A* (Fig. 62) which retain the springs, and withdraw the clutch end-plate. Bend back the locking washer and unscrew the large central nut (*see* Fig. 66). Engage top gear and apply the rear brake to prevent the gearbox main-shaft from turning. The complete clutch assembly, with the exception of the central splined sleeve, can now be withdrawn.

The central splined sleeve engages on a taper on the gearbox main-shaft and to remove it a B.S.A. extractor (Part No. 61–3362) must be used. A key locates the sleeve and this must be correctly replaced. The large central nut must be tightened very securely after properly locating the locking washer on the splined sleeve. The washer must, of course, be afterwards turned down over the flat on the nut exterior.

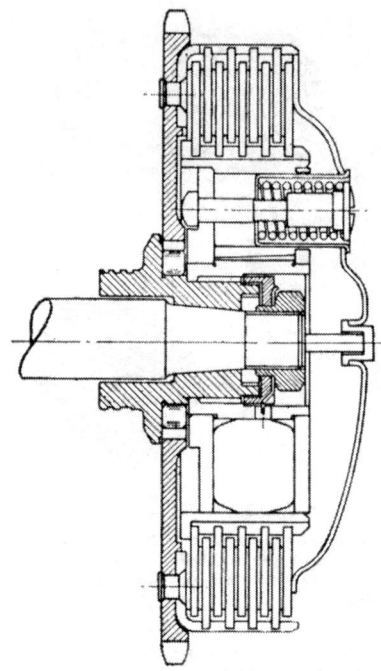

Renewing Clutch Plates (1961–6 Models B40, B40 SS90). For removal and examination of the clutch plates complete dismantling of the clutch is not necessary. The clutch hub and chain-wheel can be left in place on the gearbox main-shaft. Referring to Fig. 63, remove the four spring sleeve-nuts P and withdraw the springs and their cups. Then remove the pressure plate L, followed by the remaining plates. Withdraw the plates singly and as square as possible to avoid jamming on the chain-wheel or hub. Inspect the plates carefully. The steel plates should be smooth; if scored they should be renewed. The segments on the four driving plates are bonded in position and replacement is generally unnecessary until a big mileage has been covered. New segments are $\frac{1}{32}$ in. thick. If the segments are glazed or show signs of burning, or are excessively worn, renewal is called for.

FIG. 66. SECTIONED VIEW OF B.S.A. CLUTCH ASSEMBLY (1958–60)

Applies to the O.H.V. Models B31, B33.

Complete Dismantling of the Clutch (1961–6 Models B40, B40 SS90). Remove the oil-bath chain case cover and the clutch plates as previously described. Then remove the engine sprocket, chain and chain-wheel as a unit. The chain is of the "endless" type and has no spring link. Before the engine sprocket can be removed the alternator must be withdrawn. Disconnect its leads outside the chain case by means of the snap connectors.

Note the cable colours and draw the lead through the grommet in the back of the chain case.

Remove the three nuts and washers shown at *E* in Fig. 63 and withdraw the stator which houses the coils. The slipper type chain tensioner which pivots on the stator studs can then be removed. Note the location of the distance-pieces. The rotor, which rotates, is keyed to the engine mainshaft. Straighten the tab of the locking washer *B* and remove nut *C* which has a right-hand thread. When doing this engage top gear and apply the rear brake. Then withdraw the rotor. Be careful not to lose its key.

The centre sleeve on which the clutch is mounted is fitted to a tapered mainshaft and secured by the central nut. Straighten the tab on its washer

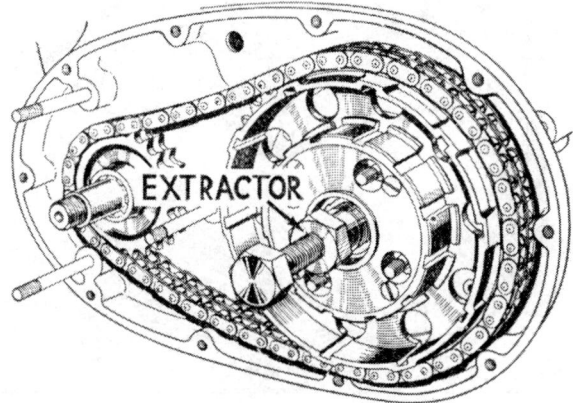

FIG. 67. USING B.S.A. EXTRACTOR FOR FINAL DISMANTLING OF 1961–6 B.S.A. CLUTCH

and remove the nut. Engage top gear and apply the rear brake to facilitate removal if necessary. Now withdraw the clutch push-rod from the centre of the mainshaft. To remove the centre sleeve from the mainshaft taper use the B.S.A. extractor, tool No. 61–3583. Screw the extractor (*see* Fig. 67) into the centre sleeve as far as possible and then screw in the extractor bolt until it contacts the end of the mainshaft. A sharp blow on the spanner applied to the extractor bolt should free the clutch centre from the shaft. The clutch minus its plates, the primary chain, and the engine sprocket can now be drawn off together. Unscrew the extractor and remove the clutch hub containing the rubber shock-absorbers. Examine the eight rubbers and remove only if wear or damage is suspected (*see* page 121).

Primary Chain Adjustment (Models with Plunger Type Rear Suspension). At 2,000-mile intervals detach the inspection cover from the oil-bath chain case and check the tension of the primary chain. This chain should have a total up-and-down movement at the centre of the chain run of about ½ in., with the chain in its tightest position (obtained by slowly turning the engine). On all models retensioning is effected by drawing the gearbox backwards.

To adjust (except S.A. models), first slacken the two large nuts beneath the gearbox on the offside. These nuts are shown at *D* in Fig. 59. On

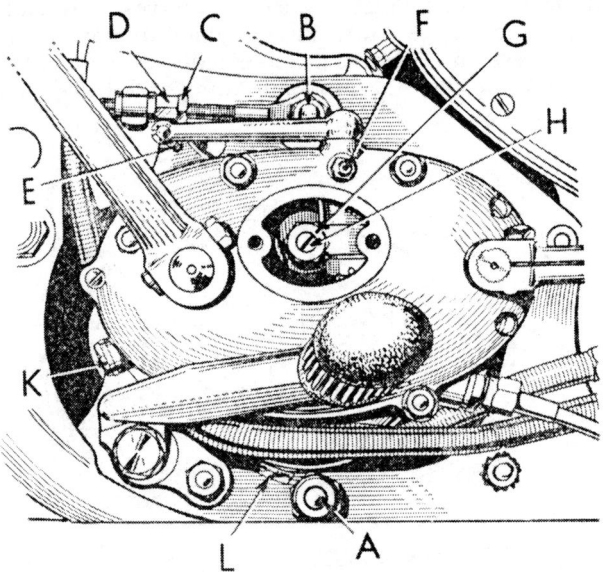

FIG. 68. CLUTCH AND PRIMARY CHAIN ADJUSTMENT ON 1955-60 "SWINGING ARM" MODELS

1955-8 "M" models the large nut on the rear fixing bolt (to which the adjuster is attached) is located on the near-side and can be loosened with a set spanner. The large nut on the front fixing bolt, however, is in a somewhat inaccessible position on the off-side. To loosen it, you must employ a long $\frac{5}{16}$-in. W. box spanner and tommy-bar. Then move the gearbox to the rear as required; to do this tighten the adjuster shown at *E* in Fig. 59. After adjusting the primary-chain tension, be careful to re-tighten the two large gearbox securing-nuts. Also check the tension of the secondary chain which is certain to have been altered by the adjustment of the primary chain.

Primary Chain Adjustment (1955-60 "Swinging Arm" Models). About every 2,000 miles remove the inspection cover shown at *C* in Fig. 28 from the oil-bath chain case. Check the tension of the primary chain by moving the chain up and down. The chain is correctly adjusted when it has ½ in. total up and down movement at its tightest point. Slowly rotate, the engine and check the tension of the chain in the centre of the chain-run with the chain in several positions. Where an adjustment is necessary, this is effected by pivoting the gearbox about its lower support bolt.

To make a primary chain adjustment on 1955-60 "swinging arm" (S.A.) models, first (see Fig. 68) loosen the large lock-nuts (A) and (B). Nut (B) also secures the adjuster in position. Then loosen the lock-nut (C) on the adjuster, and to tighten the primary chain turn the adjuster (D) *clockwise* as required to pivot the gearbox backwards the necessary amount. Finally tighten the lock-nut (C) and nuts (A) and (B). Afterwards check the tension of the secondary chain.

Primary Chain Adjustment (1961-6 "Swinging Arm" Models). On Models B40, B40 SS90 with unit construction of the engine and gearbox wear of the pre-stretched duplex type chain occurs very slowly provided the oil-bath chain case is regularly topped-up with engine oil. As may be seen in Fig. 63, an adjustable slipper type tensioner is included for the lower chain run. On a new machine it is advisable to check and if necessary adjust the tension of the primary chain after covering 2,000 miles. Subsequently this can be done at longer intervals.

To check chain tension and make an adjustment it is necessary to remove the oil-bath chain case cover as described on page 96. The tension of the primary chain is correct when there is approximately ⅛ in. free play in the top run midway between the sprockets with the chain in its tightest position. If an adjustment is necessary, slacken the two lower nuts which secure the stator. These nuts are shown at E in Fig. 63. The position of the slipper type tensioner can then be altered as required. Primary chain adjustment does not, of course, affect secondary chain adjustment as on pre-1961 models.

Secondary Chain Adjustment (Plunger-type Spring-Frame "B," "M" Series Models). On plunger models, check the tension of the secondary chain about every 1,000 miles and effect an adjustment if the chain has stretched. An adjustment is also called for if the primary chain has been re-tensioned. To check the adjustment, place the machine on its central stand so that the wheel is in the lowest position and note whether the total up-and-down movement at the centre of the bottom run, with the chain in its tightest position, is correct. This movement should be about half an inch.

To re-tension the secondary chain, with the machine on its central stand, slacken off the hand adjuster for the rear brake. Then slacken hexagon A (*see* Fig. 69) with the appropriate spanner, and with a tommy-bar applied at C, loosen the spindle. Next loosen the hexagon B on the near-side

spindle end, and then with a screwdriver or spanner screw the adjusters
D evenly in or out as required, to obtain the correct chain tension. Finally
re-tighten hexagons *B, A*; adjust rear brake, and check wheel alignment.

Secondary Chain Adjustment (1955–60 "Swinging Arm" Models). Check
the tension of the secondary chain about every 1,000 miles, with the

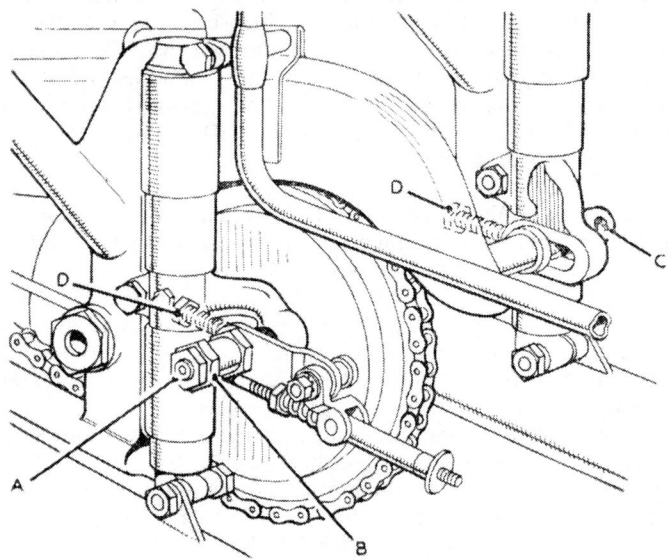

FIG. 69. SECONDARY CHAIN ADJUSTMENT ON PLUNGER-TYPE
SPRING-FRAME "B" AND "M" MODELS

machine on its central stand and the chain in its tightest position. Where
a chain case is fitted, remove the two rubber plugs.

Referring to Fig. 76, unscrew slightly with a tommy-bar or a spanner
(1956–60) the spindle (*B*) and then loosen the hexagon on the near side of
the wheel hub. Slacken the lock-nuts (*D*) and screw the adjusters (*E*)
evenly in or out as required until the chain has in its tightest position a
total up-and-down movement (whip) of 1¼ in. at the centre of the bottom
chain run. If in doubt as to the alignment of the wheels, it is advisable to
check their alignment (*see* page 108) after adjusting the secondary chain.

Secondary Chain Adjustment (1961–6 "Swinging Arm" Models). On
Models B40, B40 SS90 check the secondary chain tension about every
2,000 miles with the machine on its stand and the rear wheel in its lowest
position. Turn the rear wheel slowly until you find the chain in its tightest

position and then check the total up and down movement in the centre of the chain run. This should be 1⅛ in.

If a secondary chain adjustment is necessary, adjustment should be made in the following manner. Referring to Fig. 70, slacken the two spindle nuts *B*, both nuts securing the anchor strap *D*, and the knurled adjuster nut *A* on the rod operating the rear brake. Then pull the rear wheel backwards as required by tightening the two adjuster nuts *C* until the tension of the chain is found to be correct. It is important to tighten both adjuster nuts the *same amount* to avoid upsetting the alignment of the front and rear wheels. After making the necessary adjustment tighten firmly the two nuts securing the anchor strap *D*. Also tighten firmly the

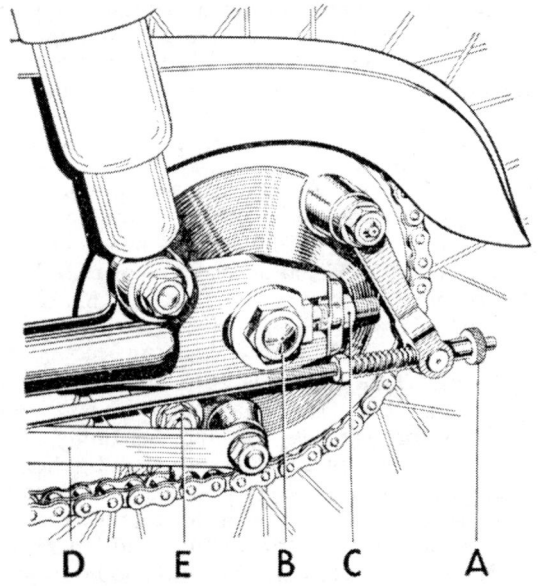

FIG. 70. SECONDARY CHAIN ADJUSTMENT ON 1961–6
"SWINGING ARM" MODELS B40 AND B40 SS90

two spindle nuts *B* and turn the adjuster nut *A* on the rear brake rod until brake adjustment is such that the rear wheel can spin freely but is locked quickly on applying the rear brake pedal. If in any doubt after secondary chain adjustment, check the wheel alignment as described on page 108.

Primary Chain-case Removal (1955–60 "Swinging Arm" Models). To withdraw the outer cover from the aluminium oil-bath chain case (*see* Fig. 28) it is only necessary to remove the near-side footrest and the fifteen cover-securing screws. Prior to any further dismantling, remove the engine sprocket and the clutch. The back half of the chain case is secured to the crankcase by three bolts behind the engine sprocket. Remove these three bolts after breaking the locking wire passed through the heads of the bolts. Also remove the single bolt at the rear of the case.

Chain Stretch. It is advisable to renew immediately any primary or secondary chain when the stretch exceeds a quarter of an inch per foot. To test for stretch, close up a foot length of the chain, measure the length, pull the links apart, and measure the length again. The difference between the two lengths is the amount the chain has stretched.

Gearbox Repairs. It is not recommended that the average B.S.A. owner should strip down his gearbox completely and attempt major repairs. Considerable experience and skill are needed to do this work which is best entrusted to the makers or a B.S.A. repair specialist.

TYRES, WHEELS, AND BRAKES

To Obtain Good Tyre Mileage. Always maintain the correct tyre pressures and keep the wheels in alignment. Avoid fierce acceleration, violent braking, and stunt cornering. Handle the clutch gently, remove flints which bed into the cover, and keep oil or paraffin from the treads. Fit a rubber tube to the breather pipe and position so that any oil emerging drips clear of the wheel track.

Maintaining Correct Tyre Pressures. Over-inflation causes vibration, strains the cover, and can cause concussion bursts; under-inflation produces a tendency for tyre creep, rolling, instability of steering, and cracking of the cover. All of these things are objectionable and you should therefore always run with the tyres inflated to the correct pressures and check the pressures weekly with a pressure gauge.

The correct inflation pressures for all 1955 and later solo models are given in Table III, and these recommendations should be strictly adhered to. Where a pillion passenger is carried, it is usually advisable to add at least 7 lb per sq in. to the solo rider rear-type pressure. Make a practice of inspecting the front and rear tyres weekly for embedded flints and cuts. This often saves a puncture, and takes far less time to attend to!

Concerning Tyre Pressure Tables. Note that the tyre pressure recommendations given in Table III are correct for a rider weighing not more than 140 lb. If you are heavier than 140 lb, or carry a pillion passenger, heavy luggage, or have any doubt about tyre pressures, use the tyre pressures in accordance with Table IV which shows the minimum pressures recommended for individual tyres subjected to specified loads.

TABLE III

CORRECT TYRE PRESSURES FOR 1955–66, PLUNGER,
AND "SWINGING ARM" MODELS (SOLO)

(Shown in lb per sq in.)*

Model .	B31	B32	B33	B34	B40	B40	M33
Front .	17	20	17	22	17	17	17
Rear .	23	16	19	16	21	21	19

Where the load is abnormal, the most satisfactory method of deter-
mining the correct tyre pressures is to take or ride the B.S.A. to the nearest
weighbridge (provided at most large transport depots and railway stations)
and check individually the fully laden weight with passenger seated,
on the front and rear tyre. Then consult Table IV for the recommended
tyre pressures.

Mending Punctures. On some spring-frame models with quickly-
detachable wheels a portion of the rear mudguard is hinged to facilitate

TABLE IV

MINIMUM TYRE PRESSURES FOR SPECIFIC LOADS

Nominal Tyre Section (Inches)	Inflation Pressures—lb per sq in.					
	16	18	20	24	28	32
	Load per Tyre—lb					
2·375	120	140	160	185	210	240
2·50	120	140	160	185	210	240
2·75	140	160	180	210	250	280
3·00	160	180	200	240	300	350
3·25	200	240	280	350	400	440
3·50	280	320	350	400	450	500
4·00	360	400	430	500	—	—

(By Courtesy of The Dunlop Rubber Co., Ltd.)

* On "swinging arm" and plunger-type spring-frame models where a solo
rider exceeds 140 lb in weight, it is advisable to increase the front tyre pressure
by 1 lb per sq in. for every 28 lb above 140 lb. For the rear tyre the pressure
increase should be 1 lb per sq in. for every 14 lb increase above 140 lb.

rear wheel removal; on other models part of the rear guard is detachable. The hinged or detachable portion is held by the lower rear-chain stays. Wheel removal is dealt with in later paragraphs.

When removing a cover with tyre levers, start near the valve and push the opposite side of the cover into the base of the rim. Test for a puncture by submerging the tube in water. Clean the tube with sandpaper and rub off all dust. Next select a suitable auto-vulcanizing patch such as the "Vulcafix" and remove its linen backing. If solution is *not* used, rub the prepared face of the patch with a cloth moistened in petrol and transfer the brown deposit on the cloth to the punctured area. Repeat this operation and allow the patch and transferred deposit to dry for one minute. If solution *is* used, apply it to the *tube only* and allow it to become "tacky."

FIG. 71. CHECKING WHEEL ALIGNMENT ON A SOLO

The straight-edge should contact the tyres at four points. Before checking the alignment, see that the rear wheel is hard up against the adjusters.

Now affix the patch to the tube, using slight pressure, particularly at the edges, and apply french chalk.

Alignment of Wheels. In order to obtain maximum tyre life and good steering, the wheels must always be kept in perfect alignment. Moving the rear wheel in order to re-tension the secondary chain may upset the alignment.

If desired, it is easy to check the alignment of the motor-cycle wheels by placing a straight-edge or board alongside the two wheels, with the handlebars in their normal position. It should, of course, touch the tyres at *four* points, with the handlebars "square."*

Some riders use a taut piece of string attached to an anchorage post. Where a sidecar is fitted, the sidecar wheel should "toe-in" to the extent of about ¾ in. (*see* Fig. 72) and the motor-cycle itself should *lean slightly*

* Assuming, of course, that the tyres are of the same section. If the rear tyre is of larger section than the front one, due allowance must be made.

outwards away from the sidecar. The exact dimensions vary slightly according to the design of sidecar fitted, and the maker's instructions should be closely followed.

To Remove Front Wheel (1955 Model B33, 1956-8 "M" Models). First remove the nut (*C*, Fig. 73) securing the lower end of the brake anchorage-strap to the brake cover-plate. Also loosen the nuts securing the upper end of the strap. Next disconnect the brake-cam operating

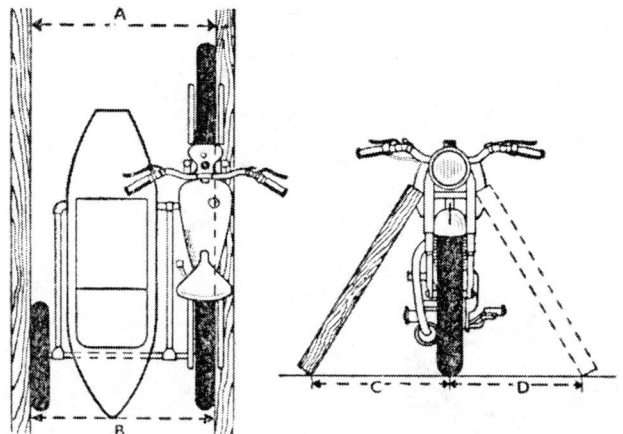

Fig. 72. Checking Wheel Adjustment of a Side-car Outfit

If adjustment is correct, dimension *A* is about ⅞ in. less than dimension *B*, and dimension *C* about 1 in. more than dimension *D*.

lever, and then detach the cable by unscrewing the adjustable cable-stop from the bracket.

Now, referring to Fig. 73, slacken the pinch-bolt *A* and unscrew *clockwise* the wheel spindle *B* with a tommy-bar inserted through the hole in the end of the spindle which has a left-hand thread. While supporting the weight of the wheel, withdraw the spindle from the near-side and remove the wheel. No distance-tube is provided on the near-side, but a bush projects from the brake-drum side of the hub. Do not allow the wheel to fall over on to this bush. Although the bush is pressed in, a sharp blow on it may force the bush back into the hub. The remedy in this case is to retrieve and re-position the bush by means of the front-wheel spindle.

To Remove Front Wheel (1956-7 "B" Models). Referring to Fig. 73, to remove the front wheel, first remove the nut (*C*) from the brake cover-plate; also disconnect the brake cable. Now slacken the pinch-bolt (*A*) and remove the nut (*E*) on the opposite side. It has a normal right-hand thread. Then with a tommy-bar inserted into the hole on the head of the wheel spindle (*B*), pull the spindle out. When doing this, support the weight of the front wheel. As the spindle emerges, pull the wheel away from the off-side fork leg and remove it. Be careful not to allow the wheel to fall on the bush projecting from the brake-drum side.

When replacing the front wheel, see that all nuts and the pinch-bolt (*A*) are firmly re-tightened. *Before* tightening the pinch-bolt and *after* tightening the spindle nut (*E*), it is essential to depress the forks once or twice to enable the near-side fork end to position itself on the spindle shank.

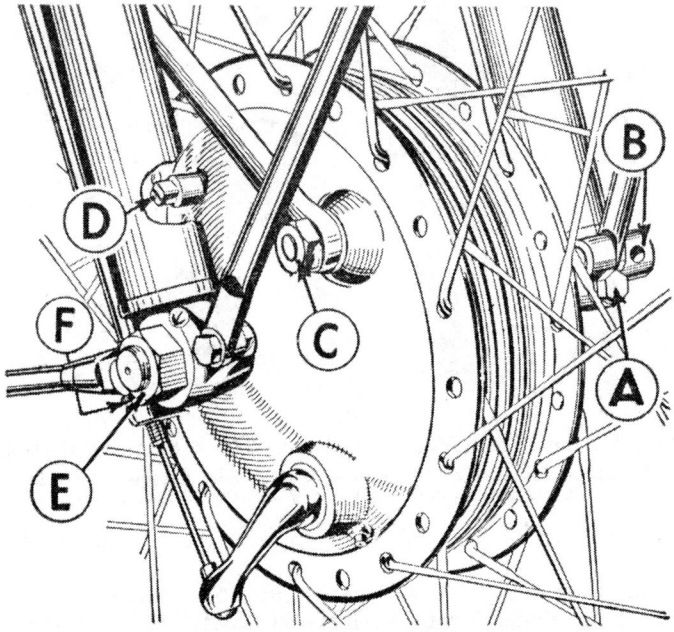

Fig. 73. Front Wheel Removal and Brake Adjustment
(1956–7 "B" Models)

On late 1956–7 models the front brake has a modified cam and a
detachable cam-operating lever.

Failure to observe this precaution may cause the near-side fork leg to be clamped out of position, thereby preventing the forks from functioning correctly.

To Remove Front Wheel (1958–60 "B" Models). Referring to Fig. 74, first disconnect the front brake cable. Then remove the four bolts *A* which secure the caps to the bottom ends of the telescopic fork legs. It is then possible to withdraw the wheel from the machine.

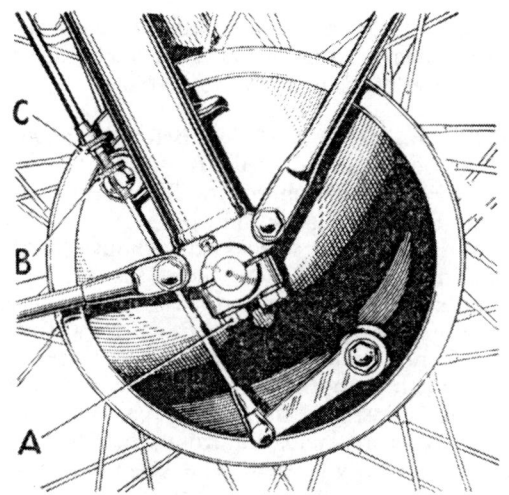

FIG. 74. FRONT WHEEL REMOVAL AND BRAKE ADJUSTMENT
(1958–60 "B" MODELS)

At *B* and *C* are shown the lock-nut and adjuster for the front brake.

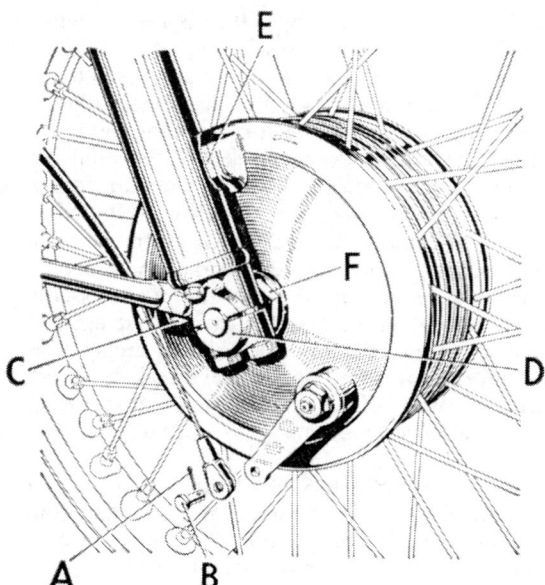

FIG. 75. FRONT WHEEL REMOVAL ON 1961–6 MODELS B40 AND B40 SS90

Replace the front wheel in the reverse order of removal. Note that it is most important to engage properly the brake anchorage peg on the off-side fork leg with the slot in the brake cover plate.

Front Wheel Removal (1961-6 Models B40, B40 SS90). Place a box beneath the crankcase so as to raise the front wheel clear of the ground. Then, referring to Fig. 75, disconnect the front brake cable at the lever on the brake plate by removing the split pin *A* and the pivot pin *B*. On later models remove the pivot screw and locknut. Then withdraw the cable from its abutment *C* on the lower end of the fork leg. The cable is a push-fit in the abutment. Now remove the caps *D* which secure the wheel spindle to the front fork legs. When removing the four cap retaining bolts support the front wheel by hand to avoid damage.

When operating the front brake, rotation of the brake plate is prevented by the tongue *E* on the inside of the fork leg registering with a slot on the brake shoe plate. When replacing the front wheel it is important to see that the tongue *E* is correctly located. The wheel must also be positioned so that the spindle nut *F* is firmly against the R.H. fork end with no clearance between the spindle nut *F* and the end cap *D*. Tighten the four cap retaining bolts securely and finally connect up the front brake cable. Renew the split pin (where fitted) if it is damaged.

To Remove the Rear Wheel (Plunger-type Spring-Frame "B" and "M" Models). On "B" and "M" models having the *plunger* type rear suspension the rear wheel is *always* of the quickly-detachable type, and its removal is perfectly straightforward. Disconnect the tail-lamp cable connexion, assuming that a touring form of rear mudguard is provided, and remove the nuts and bolts which secure the mudguard to the rear stays (slacken nuts, later models). Then lift the rear portion of the guard upwards about its hinge, so that it is well clear of the wheel.

Referring to Fig. 69, undo the outer nut *A* on the near-side extremity of the rear-wheel spindle, using the appropriate spanner. Do not touch nut *B* (the inner nut retains the whole of the brake assembly and should not be disturbed). Now with a suitable tommy-bar applied to the hole *C* in the off-side extremity of the spindle, pull out the spindle. Remove the distance piece between the hub and wheel bracket, withdraw the wheel sideways from its driving splines, and draw it out to the rear. Note that some models have a re-designed brake cover plate with no distance piece.

To Remove the Rear Wheel (1955-60 "Swinging Arm" Models). The rear wheel is of the quickly-detachable type and has ball journal-type non-adjustable bearings. Referring to Fig. 76, to remove the rear wheel, first jack the machine up on its central stand.

On models with full-width light-alloy rear hub, remove the nut (*A*) so as to free the brake anchor-strap. Also disconnect, as shown, the rear-brake operating cable (*F*). Remove the four nuts (*G*) which secure the light-alloy hub to the boss of the chain sprocket. These nuts are accessible on the near-side, and on machines provided with a chain case can be removed individually with a box spanner after first withdrawing the rubber plug (the rear one).

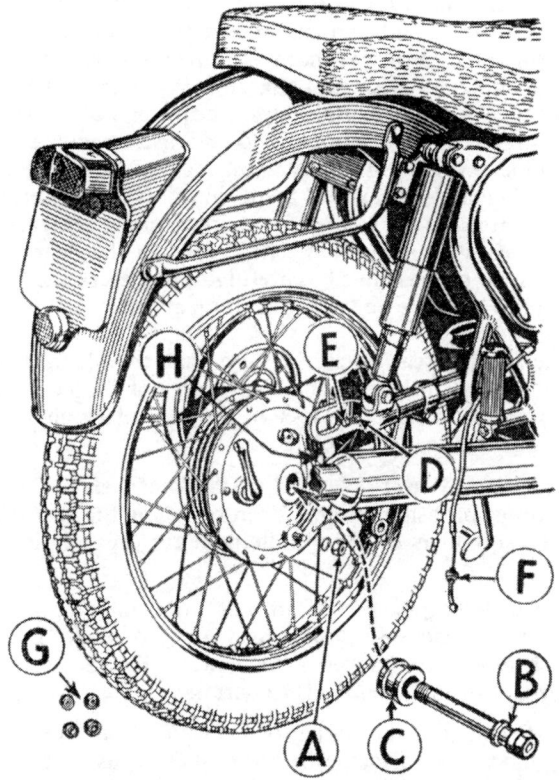

FIG. 76. SECONDARY CHAIN ADJUSTMENT, AND REMOVAL OF
QUICKLY-DETACHABLE REAR WHEEL (1956–60 MODELS)

On 1955 "B" models the hub is not of the full-width type and the brake drum is
on the opposite side, the hub being located on the drum and sprocket assembly by
splines; on the pre-1956 machines spindle *B* has a hole for tommy-bar application
but no hexagon.

Now on all models apply a tommy-bar (1955) or spanner (1956–60) to the end of the rear-wheel spindle (*B*), and unscrew it *anti-clockwise* until it can be pulled clear. Remove the distance-piece (*C*), ease the hub to the off-side until it clears the brake drum (1955) or the sprocket boss (1956–60), and withdraw the wheel downwards and to the rear.

Note that when removing the rear wheel on all models, *do not disturb the large nut on the near-side*; this nut secures the brake drum or sprocket (1956–60). Also note, when replacing the rear wheel on 1956–60 models, that it is extremely important to *tighten firmly the four nuts securing the light-alloy hub to the sprocket boss.*

Rear Wheel Removal (1961–6 B40 and B40 SS90 Models). Place the machine on its centre stand and disconnect the secondary chain by removing its spring link. When withdrawing the secondary chain from the rear brake drum make sure that the chain remains on the gearbox sprocket. Referring to Fig. 70, remove the knurled adjuster nut *A* from the rear brake rod. Also remove the anchor arm *D* and disconnect the speedometer cable at its union on the worm drive housing. Now unscrew the wheel spindle nuts *B* to enable the wheel to be withdrawn rearwards from the "swinging arm" fork ends. Withdraw it from under the off-side of the rear mudguard after canting the machine over to the near side. When the rear wheel is out of the frame be careful not to disturb the setting of the chain adjusters *C*, otherwise wheel alignment must be checked after assembly.

When replacing the rear wheel be sure that the chain adjusters are pressed firmly against the fork ends. Also do not forget to replace the hairpin spring on the connecting link of the secondary chain so that its closed end faces the direction of chain movement.

Replacing the Rear Wheel ("B," "C," "M" Models). The procedure is the reverse order of dismantling. When replacing the rear wheel, make certain that the shoulders of the spindle nuts are properly located in the rear-fork ends.

The Wheel Bearings. The front and rear wheel hubs have ball journal bearings and no adjustment is necessary or provided. During initial assembly the bearings are packed with grease. This is sufficient until a complete overhaul of the machine is undertaken.

Brake Adjustment. For the benefit of yourself, your "next of kin," and the general public, always maintain the brakes so as to give maximum leverage and efficiency. With the brakes correctly adjusted the shoes should be just clear of the drums when the brakes are off, and close enough for immediate contact when the brakes are applied. Adjustment of the rear brake is by means of a thumb-nut at the rear end of the brake rod. Front brake adjustment is by means of a knurled thumb-nut on the cable stop, fitted to the front forks or front brake cover-plate. On 1961–6 models the front brake adjustment is at the handlebars. The 1955 "B" models have an adjustable stop for setting the rear-brake pedal to the most advantageous position; adjust this before adjusting the brake rod.

Many 1956–60 "B" models have a brake-shoe adjustment in addition to knurled finger adjusters. The latter are designed for cable adjustment during *initial assembly.* All subsequent brake adjustments should be effected at the brake-shoe fulcrums shown at (*H*) and (*D*) in Figs. 76 and 73 respectively. To compensate for wear of the brake linings (front or rear), apply a screwdriver or a small spanner to the fulcrum adjuster-pin (e.g. (*D*), Fig. 73), and turn *clockwise.* A series of clicks is audible as the adjuster pin is turned; each click corresponds to *one-twelfth of a turn.* To ensure correct brake adjustment, turn the adjuster pin fully clockwise, and then turn back until the front or rear wheel is just able to spin freely.

If grease gets on brake linings, remove the shoes and wash the linings in

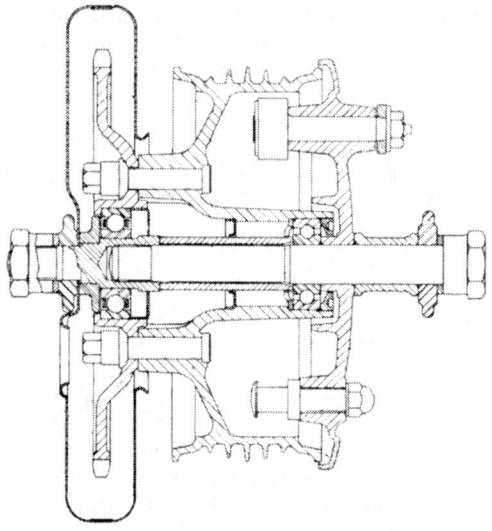

Fig. 77. Rear Hub Arranangement on Models B31, B33

petrol. If the linings become glazed, roughen with a wire brush or a file. Do not adjust brakes too closely, as this will cause friction and heat, and possibly cause the grease in the hubs to melt, quite apart from impairing performance.

About every 2,000 miles check the tightness of the lock-nut on the brake cover-plate on 1955 "B" models and "M" models with 7-in. brakes. In the case of the 7-in. brakes, occasional centralizing is desirable. Loosen the lock-nut on the brake cover-plate so as to slacken the fulcrum pin in its slotted hole. Then apply the brake, when the fulcrum pin will automatically centralize the assembly. Now with the brake kept on, re-tighten the lock-nut.

Removal and Replacement of Brake Shoes (1955–60 Models). With the wheel removed, slacken fully the brake-shoe adjuster, and remove the brake plate from the wheel. Then grasp the shoes firmly, pulling them outwards to allow the shoes to clear the fulcrums and come away. Replace the brake shoes in the reverse order of removal. Hook the springs on to the shoes and place the ends of the shoes in position on the fulcrum pins. Push the brake shoes outwards until they are pulled into the correct position by the springs. The springs are strong and care must be taken to avoid getting the fingers trapped during shoe assembly. Note that brake shoes with new linings fitted are obtainable through the Exchange Replacement scheme.

Renewing the Brake Shoes (1961 Onwards). Remove the wheel (*see* page 109–14) and lay the brake shoe plate on a bench. Referring to Fig. 78, take off the cam lever *A* and press the spindle *B* slightly inwards

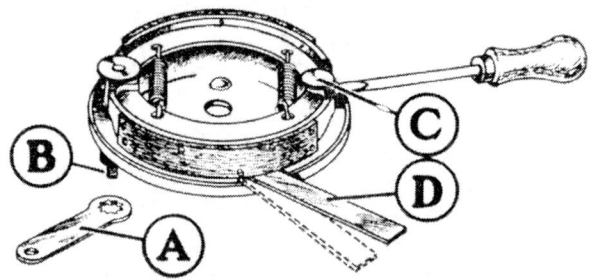

Fig. 78. Removing Brake Shoes (1961 Onwards)

allowing the shoes to become clear of the brake plate. Separate the shoes slightly with a screwdriver at fulcrum pin *C*. Then apply a lever *D* between one shoe and the brake shoe plate and prise the shoe off the plate until the spring tension is released. Both shoes can now be withdrawn.

It is hardly worth the trouble of re-lining shoes in view of the fact, that B.S.A. Motor Cycles, Ltd. through their dealers supply factory re-conditioned brake shoes. It is, of course, necessary to hand in the old shoes under the Exchange Replacement Service.

To fit the re-conditioned shoes lay the shoes on a bench and connect the springs. Position the ends of the shoes correctly on the fulcrum pin and cam lever. The shoes should form a "vee" between them, about 2 in. from the brake plate. Then with the palm of each hand resting on a shoe, press downwards and outwards until the brake shoes are pulled into position by the springs. *See* note on page 121.

After fitting rear shoes with new linings, centralizing is necessary. Replace the brake cover plate, complete with shoes, fulcrum pin and cam, in the brake drum. Slacken the fulcrum pin nut shown at *E* in Fig. 70 and turn the cam so as to expand the brake shoes in the normal manner. The fulcrum pin will then move in its housing until both shoes are pressing equally on the brake drum. Afterwards firmly tighten the fulcrum-pin nut and release the brake. Front shoes require similar treatment.

STEERING HEAD AND FRONT FORKS

Adjustment of the Steering Head (1955–60 Models). About every 2,000 miles lift the machine and place a box beneath the crankcase to raise the front wheel clear of the ground. Then check that there is no friction in the ball bearings and that no up-and-down movement is possible. Also verify that the steering is true.

Where telescopic-type front forks are fitted, unscrew the damper knob

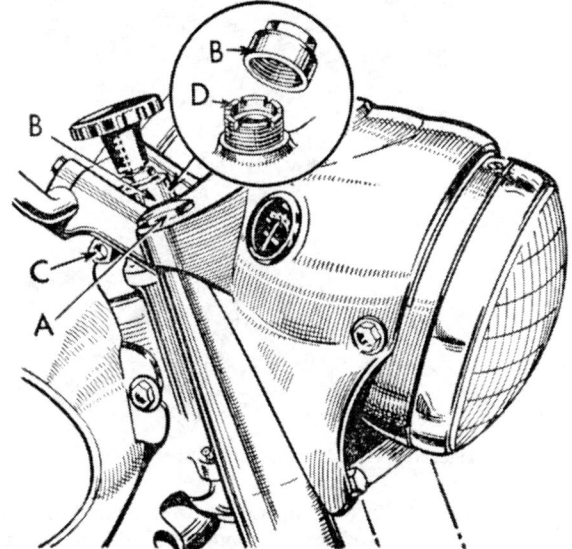

FIG. 79. STEERING HEAD ADJUSTMENT ON 1955–60 MODELS

No steering damper is fitted on 1958–60 models.

with stem where fitted, and remove the steering head top-cap shown at *B* in Fig. 79. Then loosen the clip bolt *C* and tighten the adjusting sleeve *D** until all slackness in the steering head disappears. Be sure not to over-tighten the bearings and cause stiffness. Finally, re-tighten the clip bolt *C* and fit and tighten the top cap *B*.

Steering Head Adjustment (1961 Onwards). About every 2,000 miles the steering head should be tested for play which must not be permitted. The

* The sleeve can be turned by using a hammer and a $2\frac{1}{2}$ in. length of mild steel strip 1 in. wide and $\frac{1}{16}$ in. thick. The use of a punch is likely to damage the threads.

telescopic front forks must, however, be able to rotate quite freely. Support the crankcase on a box so that the front wheel is raised clear of the ground. Then grasp the front fork legs and attempt to push them backwards and forwards. If any play exists, take this up as described below.

Referring to Fig. 80, slacken the clamping nuts C and E. and then tighten down the clamping nut D until play is removed. To check that

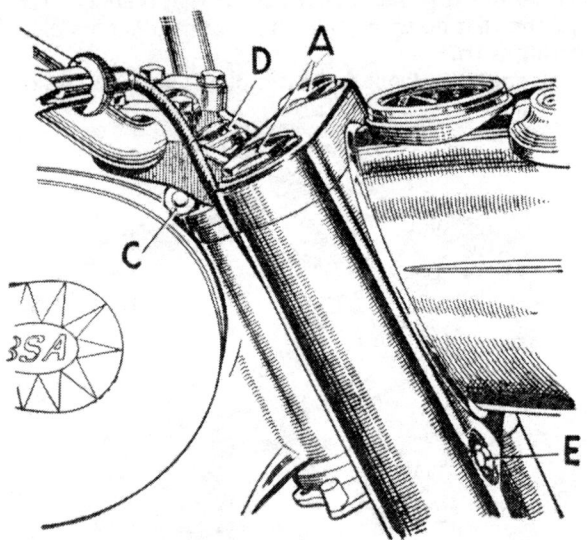

FIG. 80. STEERING HEAD ADJUSTMENT ON 1961–6 MODELS

the clamping nut has not been over tightened, move the handlebars round slowly. There must be no stiffness present, and the forks must rotate quite freely. After adjusting the steering head, firmly tighten the clamping nuts C and E. The latter clamps the fork legs and must be quite tight.

Telescopic Front Forks. 1955–66 telescopic front forks require no maintenance other than the routine checking of nuts for tightness and the replenishment of the fork legs with suitable oil (*see* page 48) after a very considerable mileage. The time when replenishment is called for is indicated by excessive up-and-down movement.

The "Swinging Arm" Rear Suspension. The self-contained hydraulic dampers require no topping-up or other maintenance, and the "swinging arm" pivots on 1955–60 models have "silentbloc" bushes requiring no lubrication (*see* page 50). The springs in each suspension unit (1955–66) are, however, adjustable for load by means of adjustable cams which can be turned to one of the three alternative positions shown in Figs. 81, 82. The normal position (set by the makers) is shown at (*A*).

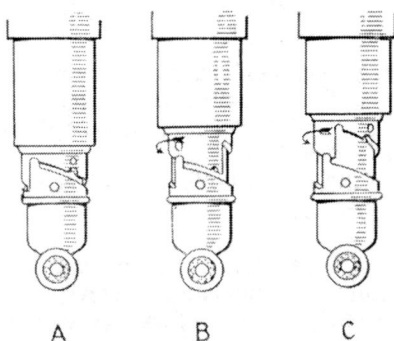

A   B   C

FIG. 81. ALTERNATIVE SPRING-LOADING ADJUSTMENTS FOR THE EARLIER "SWINGING ARM" REAR SUSPENSION UNITS (1955-7)

Progressively stiffer springing is obtained by setting the adjuster cams in the positions *A, B, C*.

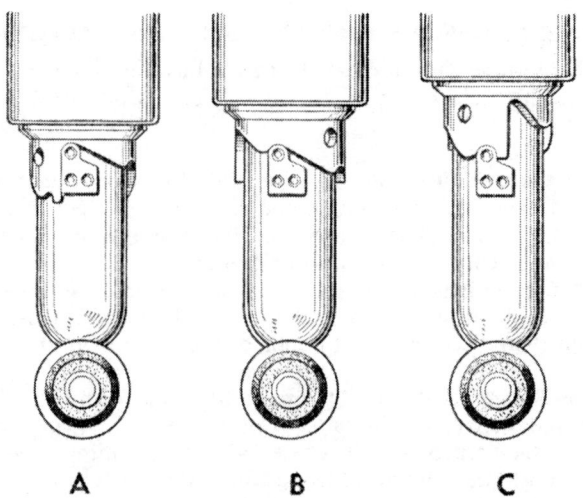

A   B   C

FIG. 82. ALTERNATIVE SPRING-LOADING ADJUSTMENT FOR THE LATER "SWINGING ARM" REAR SUSPENSION UNITS (1958-66)

Where the rider's weight is above average or the machine is being used habitually over rough terrain, slightly stiffer springing may be desirable and the required adjustment can be made in a few seconds; with the Cee-spanner in the tool kit, turn the adjuster cams to the position shown at

(*B*). Adjustment is facilitated by the application of a little thin oil. Where a pillion passenger or heavy luggage is carried, it is advisable to set the suspension unit in the highest position by turning the cams to the position shown at (*C*).

To Remove Rear Suspension Units. As previously mentioned, the hydraulic dampers require no maintenance attention whatever. During manufacture they are sealed and if they become ineffective or damaged, it is necessary to renew them.

After detaching the two pivot bolts the complete suspension units can be removed from the frame.

Replacing Fork Top Caps. Lack of alignment (especially on cowled-headlamp models) can cause difficulty in screwing home the telescopic-fork upper caps after replenishing the fork legs with oil (page 48), or after fitting windscreen brackets (as used on the "Unicorn") to the forks. Referring to Fig. 79, the remedy is to slacken the headlamp mounting bolts, and the two nuts on the fork-crown pinch-bolts, *before* tightening the caps *A*.

MISCELLANEOUS (B40 AND B40 SS90 MACHINES)

Except where otherwise indicated, the following *motor-cycle* general maintenance instructions apply to the 343 c.c. Model B40 and Model B40 SS90.

Replacing Clutch Cable (1961–6). On 1961–4 machines the timing cover has no inspection cap to facilitate the removal and replacement of the clutch operating-cable. The removal of the timing cover is necessary to give access to the cable control arm and union.

On 1965–6 machines withdraw the clutch cable as follows. Slacken right off the cable adjuster shown in Fig. 83, turn the cable-control arm *inwards*, and then disconnect both ends of the cable from the sockets.

To Adjust Clutch (1965–6). The main adjustment and the fine adjustment at the handlebars are the same as on the 1961–4 343 c.c. models, but an exposed cable-control arm is located above the timing cover as shown in Fig. 83. With the clutch adjusted correctly and engaged, the cable-control arm should be inclined *outwards* to a small extent as indicated (not the dotted line) in Fig. 83. On squeezing the handlebar clutch lever, the cable-control arm located above the timing cover should assume a position approximately parallel with the timing-cover joint face as illustrated by dotted lines in Fig. 83.

To adjust the clutch (fully engaged) in order to obtain the above-mentioned correct control-arm setting, referring to Fig. 60, after removing the inspection cover *H* loosen the lock-nut *G* and with a screwdriver turn the adjuster *F* as required. Afterwards firmly re-tighten the lock-nut *G*. Should a further *fine* adjustment be required to obtain the overall correct adjustment (a small gap as indicated in Fig. 83), make this by means of the cable adjuster shown in Fig. 83. Where only a minor clutch adjustment is

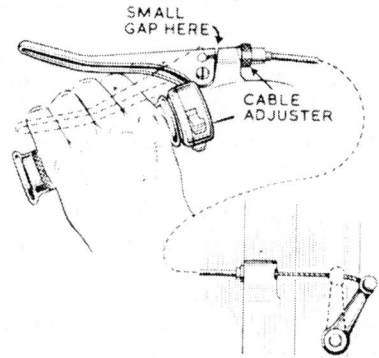

FIG. 83. THE FINE CLUTCH-CABLE ADJUSTMENT (*above*);
THE CORRECT POSITIONS OF THE CABLE-CONTROL ARM ON
1965-6 MODELS WITH THE CLUTCH ENGAGED AND DISENGAGED (*below*)

With the control arm in the dotted position the clutch is disengaged. The handlebar
adjustment (a fine adjustment) is similar to that on the 1961–4 Models B40 and
B40 SS90.

needed, this can often be effectively made without having to turn the adjuster shown at *F* in Fig. 60. If a major adjustment is necessitated, make sure that the inspection cover *H* is afterwards properly replaced.

The Clutch Cush Drive (1961–6). Should you ever have to remove the eight rubber shock-absorber segments from the clutch hub (*see* page 101), note that B.S.A. service tool 61–3689 is needed for fitting used or new rubber segments. When assembling the clutch always remember to fit: first a plain steel plate next to the chain sprocket assembly, and then *alternately* the bonded-segment and plain steel plates.

Assembling Brake Shoes (1966 Model B40 Only). With further reference to the advice given on page 116, note that on the 1966 Model B40 the front-brake shoes are of the floating type (i.e. not pivoted about a fulcrum) and the *position* of the brake lining on each brake shoe differs according to whether the latter is a leading or trailing shoe. Obviously the two shoes are not interchangeable, and must not be fitted in the wrong positions.

MISCELLANEOUS (B40 AND B40 SS90 ENGINES)

Unless otherwise stated, the following *engine* maintenance instructions apply to 343 c.c B40 and B40 SS90 types.

Oil Pump Ball-valve (1961–6). When removing and cleaning the oil sump filter (*see* pages 41–2) every 2,000 miles it is advisable also to check that the ball of the non-return valve (located in the oil pump suction-pipe), shown at *C* in Fig. 23, is quite free to move on its seating. Insert a piece of suitable wire into the valve orifice to ascertain its true condition. Failure of the ball to rise off its seating under suction results in little or no oil returning to the tank; sticking of the ball off its seating also can cause oil to pass from the tank through the pump directly into the crankcase with the engine stationary.

Oil-pressure Release Valve (1961–6). This valve shown at *D* in Fig. 23 should not be disturbed unnecessarily and it is unlikely to develop trouble. Should it be necessary to remove the valve for inspection because of an excessive alteration in the oil pressure, it is *essential* on all 1961–4 B40 and B40 SS90 343 c.c engines, prior to engines Nos. B40F–1O3 and B40SS–101 respectively, to replace or renew the coil spring with its *larger diameter* end-seating fitted inside the hexagon-headed plug. Wrong replacement of this particular coil spring will inevitably adversely affect valve functioning. On B40 and B40 SS90 engines having an engine No. as stated above, or of later manufacture, the coil spring can safely be fitted *either way round*.

Contact-breaker Gap (1965–6). The 1965–6 Lucas contact-breaker and automatic ignition-advance mechanism is of quite different design to the 1955–64 type shown in Fig. 36; also instead of its being mounted behind the cylinder barrel as shown in Fig. 23, it is of the type illustrated in Fig. 84 and is housed inside the engine timing-cover on the off side. Removal of a circular inspection cover from the latter gives immediate access to the new mechanism, and to the contacts

As in the case of the pre-1965 assembly, check and if necessary adjust the contact-breaker gap on a new or reconditioned engine after covering 500 miles and thereafter every 2,000 miles. It is advisable as far as possible to *maintain* a gap of 0·015 in. When cleaning the contacts, always check their gap *afterwards*, especially if removal of pitting with a carborundum slip becomes necessary.

To check the 1965–6 contact-breaker gap, remove the contact-breaker inspection cover, take out the sparking plug, and slowly rotate the engine forward by means of the kick-starter or rear wheel (with a gear engaged) until the pivoted contact rocker-arm heel is on the peak of the cam. Then carefully check the gap with suitable feeler gauges.

If a gap adjustment is found to be necessary, referring to Fig. 84. loosen the locking screw which secures the fixed-contact carrier plate and then move the plate clockwise or anti-clockwise as required until a gap of exactly 0·015 in. is obtained. The ignition timing of B40 and B40 SS90 engines is very sensitive to contact-breaker adjustment (*see* page 84) and this should never be neglected. Note that an excessively big or small gap advances or retards the ignition timing respectively.

When checking the contact-breaker gap also inspect the automatic ignition-advance mechanism (*see* Fig. 84) as described on page 63. Occasionally apply a few drops of thin oil to the two governor-weight pivots.

Cleaning Contact-breaker Contacts (1965–6). Clean both contacts (normally required about every 5,000 miles) as described on pages 62 and

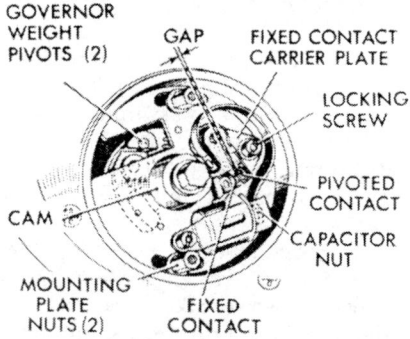

FIG. 84. DETAILS OF LUCAS CONTACT-BREAKER FITTED INSIDE THE TIMING COVER OF 1965–6 343 C.C. B40, B40 SS90 ENGINES

Observe part of the auto-advance mechanism behind the mounting plate.

63. On all B.S.A. contact-breakers cleaning is made easier and more effective by preliminary removal of the rocker arm carrying the moving contact.

To remove the rocker arm first remove the terminal nut on the capacitor (*see* Fig. 84) and withdraw the contact-breaker spring and rocker arm from its pivot. When replacing the rocker arm make certain that the insulating washer is replaced beneath the rocker-arm heel. After assembly is completed, again check the contact-breaker gap as previously described.

Dismantling and Assembling Rocker-box (1961–6). If you have occasion to dismantle the rocker-box, drive the rocker spindles out towards the *push-rod* side, using a copper drift. Carefully note the relative positions of the various washers which must not be interchanged. If you observe any ovality in the rocker-spindle holes or on the spindles themselves, the parts concerned must be renewed.

Each rocker spindle has a small oil-sealing ring and during the assembly of the rocker-box and its contents, be most careful not to damage the two above-mentioned oil-seals. Also verify when fitting each overhead rocker that it has one thrust washer at the push-rod end and *two* thrust washers, with a spring between them, at the opposite end.

Big-end Bearing Play (All 1955–66 Models). When you have occasion to remove the cylinder barrel from the crankcase make an approximate check for wear of the connecting-rod big-end bearing. With the connecting-rod in the T.D.C or B.D.C. position, grasp its upper end firmly with both hands and see if any vertical up-and-down movement is possible. There should be *no* vertical play, but 0·020 in. side play at the big-end bearing is quite normal and necessary.

Valve Timing (1961–6). Provided that the timing-gear teeth are not excessively worn and the gears are meshed with their dash timing marks aligned as shown in Fig. 58, and also assuming that the valve clearances are correct, and that the piston is at the top of its compressions stroke, the inlet and exhaust valve timing *must* be correct. The maker's valve timing should never be altered. Do not remove the timing gears unless this is essential for some reason.

Access to the timing gears involves removing the timing-case outer cover; removal (on 1965–6 343 c.c engines) of the automatic ignition-advance mechanism, the contact-breaker; removal of the inner timing-case cover, dismantling the kick-starter gears, etc.—a rather involved job described and illustrated in B.S.A. *Service Wall Chart* No. MC5 and in the appropriate B.S.A. *Workshop Manual*. If you decide to check the valve timing, fit a degree disc to the crankshaft and a piston-position indicator to the crankcase as shown in Fig. 56

Before checking the timing, set *both* valve clearances to 0·020 in. for Model B40, and 0·015 in. for Model B40 SS90 engines. These are not the running clearances (*see* page 64) which must be restored *after* a timing check.

1961–6 Valve Timings. Measured in degrees of crankshaft rotation before and after T.D.C. and B.D.C., the correct *inlet* valve timing for 1961–6 B40 engines is: I.O. 26° before T.D.C.; I.C. 70° after B.D.C. The correct B40 exhaust valve timing is: E.O. 61½° before B.D.C.; E.C. 34½° after T.D.C. The correct *inlet* valve timing for 1962–5 B40 SS90 engines is: I.O. 51° before T.D.C.; I.C. 68° after B.D.C. The correct B40 SS90 exhaust valve timing is: E.O. 78° before B.D.C.; E.C. 37° after T.D.C.

The Ignition Timing (1965–6). It is advisable for the reasons stated on page 84 to check the ignition timing after making any adjustment to the contact-breaker gap which should be maintained at 0·015 in. To check the ignition timing, use either a piston-position indicator (inserted through the plug hole) or else a degree disc and pointer attached to the crankshaft and crankcase as shown in Fig. 56. The latter is the most accurate method.

Timing is correct if the contact "break" just begins with the piston or crankshaft 0·280 in. or 33½ degrees before T.D.C. on the compression stroke, measured by the piston position or degrees of crankshaft rotation respectively. This timing is correct with the automatic ignition-advance mechanism locked in the *fully advanced* position. Fuller instructions for timing the ignition by the crankshaft degree method are given in the 1965–6 B.S.A. *Instruction Manual*. If the ignition timing is found to be incorrect, the timing can be advanced or retarded as required by slight anti-clockwise or clockwise movement respectively of the contact-breaker mounting plate (*see* Fig. 84). Its two securing nuts or screws must, of course, first be loosened.

MAJOR OVERHAUL

Those sufficiently skilled mechanically and having the necessary equipment and special service tools available should note that the following comprehensive and well-illustrated B.S.A. publications can be obtained from B.S.A. dealers and spares stockists—

1. *Workshop Service Manuals* for the 1955–60 Models B31–B34, M33.

2. A *Workshop Service Manual* for the 1961–6 Models B40 and B40 SS90, etc.

3. *Service Wall Charts* (priced at 2/2 each) for all of the B.S.A. motorcycles dealt with in this handbook. They comprise most attractive "pin-ups", of a helpful and practical nature. Postage is extra.

INDEX

OTHER MOTORCYCLE MANUALS AVAILABLE IN THIS SERIES

ARIEL WORKSHOP MANUAL 1933-1951:
All single, twin & 4 cylinder models

ARIEL (BOOK OF) MAINTENANCE & REPAIR MANUAL 1932-1939:
LF3, LF4, LG, NF3, NF4, NG, OG, VA, VA3, VA4, VB, VF3, VF4, VG,
Red Hunter LH, NH, OH, VH & Square Four 4F, 4G, 4H

BMW FACTORY WORKSHOP MANUAL R27, R28:
English, German, French and Spanish text

BMW FACTORY WORKSHOP MANUAL R50, R50S, R60, R69S:
Also includes a supplement for the USA models: R50US, R60US, R69US.
English, German, French and Spanish text

BSA TWINS (BOOK OF) 1948-1962:
All 650cc & 500cc twins

BSA SINGLES (BOOK OF) 1955-1967:
B31, B32, B33, B34 and "Star" B40 & SS90

BSA (BOOK OF) MAINTENANCE & REPAIR 1936-1939:
All Pre-War single & twin cylinder SV & OHV models through 1939
150cc, 250cc, 350cc, 500cc, 600cc, 750cc & 1,000cc

DUCATI OHC FACTORY WORKSHOP MANUAL:
160 Junior Monza, 250 Monza, 250 GT, 250 Mark 3, 250 Mach 1, 250 SCR &
350 Sebring

HONDA 250 & 305cc FACTORY WORKSHOP MANUAL:
C.72 C.77 CS.72, CS.77, CB.72, CB.77 [HAWK]

HONDA 125 & 150cc FACTORY WORKSHOP MANUAL:
C.92, CS.92, CB.92, C.95 & CA.95

HONDA 50cc FACTORY WORKSHOP MANUAL: C.100

HONDA 50cc FACTORY WORKSHOP MANUAL: C.110

HONDA (BOOK OF) MAINTENANCE & REPAIR 1960-1966:
50cc C.100, C.102, C.110 & C.114 ~ 125cc C.92 & CB.92
250cc C.72 & CB.72 ~ 305cc CB.77

LAMBRETTA (BOOK OF) MAINTENANCE & REPAIR:
125 & 150cc, all models up to 1958, except model "48".

NORTON FACTORY TWIN CYLINDER WORKSHOP MANUAL 1957-1970: *Lightweight Twins:* 250cc Jubilee, 350cc Navigator and 400cc Electra and the *Heavyweight Twins:* Model 77, 88, 88SS, 99, 99SS, Sports Special, Manxman, Mercury, Atlas, G15, P11, N15, Ranger (P11A).

NORTON (BOOK OF) MAINTENANCE & REPAIR 1932-1939: All Pre-War SV, OHV and OHC models: 16H, 16I, 18, 19, 20, 50, 55, ES2, CJ, CSI, International 30 & 40

SUZUKI 200 & 250cc FACTORY WORKSHOP MANUAL: 250cc T20 [X-6 Hustler] ~ 200cc T200 [X-5 Invader & Sting Ray Scrambler]

SUZUKI 250cc FACTORY WORKSHOP MANUAL: 250cc ~ T10

TRIUMPH (BOOK OF) MAINTENANCE & REPAIR 1935-1939: All Pre-War single & twin cylinder models: L2/1, 2/1, 2/5, 3/1, 3/2, 3/5, 5/1, 5/2, 5/3, 5/4, 5/5, 5/10, 6/1, Tiger 70, 80, 90 & 2H. Tiger 70C, 3S & 3H, Tiger 80C & 5H, Tiger 90C, 6S, 2HC & 3SC, 5T Speed Twin & 5S and T100 Tiger 100

TRIUMPH 1937-1951 WORKSHOP MANUAL (A. St. J. Masters): Covers rigid frame and sprung hub single cylinder SV & OHV and twin cylinder OHV pre-war, military, and post-war models

TRIUMPH 1945-1955 FACTORY WORKSHOP MANUAL NO.11: Covers pre-unit, twin-cylinder rigid frame, sprung hub, swing-arm and 350cc, 500cc & 650cc.

VESPA (BOOK OF) MAINTENANCE & REPAIR 1946-1959: All 125cc & 150cc models including 42/L2 & Gran Sport

VINCENT WORKSHOP MANUAL 1935-1955: All Series A, B & C Models

COMING SOON IN THIS SAME SERIES:

BRIDGESTONE FACTORY WORKSHOP MANUAL: 50 Sport, 60 Sport, 90 De Luxe, 90 Trail, 90 Mountain, 90 Sport, 175 Dual Twin & Hurricane

BRITISH MILITARY MAINTENANCE & REPAIR MANUAL: Service & Repair data for all British WD motorcycles

BRITISH MOTORCYCLE ENGINES: AJS, Ariel, BSA, Excelsior, JAP, Norton, Royal Enfield, Rudge, Scott, Sunbeam, Triumph, Velocette, Villiers & Vincent

CEZETTA 175cc MODEL 501 SCOOTER MANUAL & PARTS BOOK

VILLIERS ENGINE WORKSHOP MANUAL: All Villiers engines through 1947

Lightning Source UK Ltd.
Milton Keynes UK
UKOW05f0020110914

238389UK00018B/1033/P